MODERN LOCOMOTIVES

HIGH-HORSEPOWER DIESELS   1966–2000

BRIAN SOLOMON

MBI Publishing Company

DEDICATION

To all my friends in the railroad industry

———————◆———————

First published in 2002 by MBI Publishing Company, Galtier Plaza, Suite 200, 380 Jackson Street, St. Paul, MN 55101-3885 USA

MBI Publishing Company books are also available at discounts in bulk quantity for industrial or sales-promotional use. For details write to Special Sales Manager at Motorbooks International Wholesalers & Distributors, Galtier Plaza, Suite 200, 380 Jackson Street, St. Paul, MN 55101-3885 USA

Library of Congress Cataloging-in-Publication Data Available

ISBN 0-7603-1258-3

Edited by Dennis Pernu
Page layout by Chris Fayers, Morwenstow, Cornwall

On the front cover: Burlington Northern Santa Fe DASH 9 No. 1116 leads an eastbound freight at Sais, New Mexico. *Photo by Brian Solomon*

On the endpaper: Detail of a freshly shopped wheel on a Southern Pacific Electro-Motive GP60. The markings "DEN 8-96" represent SP's former Rio Grande Burnham Shops in Denver. *Photo by Brian Solomon*

On the frontispiece: A Chicago & North Western SD50 and SD60 lead coal empties across the Kate Shelley High Bridge west of Boone, Iowa, in the summer of 1989. *Photo by Brian Solomon*

On the title page: First light at Bond, Maryland, on the legendary 17-Mile Grade finds a pair of CSX SD50s leading a heavily laden coal train toward Cumberland, Maryland, from the mines of West Virginia. The old Baltimore & Ohio "West End" features a succession of tough grades that still challenge the capabilities of modern motive power. *Photo by Brian Solomon*

On the back cover: Conrail's NHSE (New Haven to Selkirk) at Springfield, Massachusetts. *Photo by Brian Solomon.*

Printed in Hong Kong

CONTENTS

ACKNOWLEDGMENTS

It's always exciting to experience powerful locomotives at work, whether you are riding in the cab, pulling the throttle, or just watching them pass by. Although I do not work for a railroad or a locomotive manufacturer, I've been fortuitous in my firsthand experience with diesel locomotives. In more than two dozen years of close observation of railroad operations, I have watched and photographed powerful modern diesels everywhere from New England to California. I've variously studied new C32-8s, SD80MACs, and AC6000CWs climbing the Boston & Albany grades in western Massachusetts, enjoyed listening to SD40s, SD45s, and Tunnel Motors ascending Donner Pass, and watched the sand fly from SD70MACs lifting Powder River coal up Wyoming's Logan Hill.

This book was made possible by melding my own experiences with information obtained from many sources. I did not discover locomotives on my own, and for every step of the way through my learning process I am grateful for those who directed my interest, answered my questions, lent their expertise, and traveled with me to the far corners of the railroad world.

My father, Richard Jay Solomon, was the source of my original railway interest and has continued to support my fascination over the years. My brother Seán has accompanied me on a number of railroad trips. My mother, Maureen, has tolerated these enterprises admirably.

Among my many traveling companions on photography trips, thanks to Brian Jennison for visits to the Sierra, Tehachapi, Oregon's Blue Mountains, and trips in New England and eastern Canada; the Hoovers for visits in New England, Pennsylvania, West Virginia, Colorado, California, and the Western deserts; J. D. Schmid for trips to document the Southern Pacific and for giving me an appreciation for the sounds of dynamic brakes and EMD's 20-cylinder 645 engine; Mike Danneman for helping me explore the Midwest; Tom Danneman for trips to the Burlington Northern, especially the Mississippi River Line and its Powder River operations; Tim Doherty for trips along the Southern Tier and to Vermont to seek out Vermont Railway's GP60s; and Mike Gardner for trips here, there, and everywhere in the Northeast, but especially in Pennsylvania (also, thanks for the extensive use of his black-and-white darkroom facilities).

I also want to thank Joe McMillan for a snowy adventure on the Front Range; Mel Patrick for visits to Colorado, desert trips in Utah and Nevada, and for his great photographic expertise; Patrick Yough for trips along Metro-North and elsewhere; George Pitarys for trips in New England and Canada; Will Holloway and Brad Hellman for helping me with the intricacies of Sand Patch; Mike Abalos for elaborate, fast-paced, and detailed tours of Chicago; Doug Eisele for trips to the Southern Tier and Buffalo; Paul Hammond for driving in pursuit of an SD45; Mark Hemphill for a trip along the Illinois Central; and Blair Kooistra for trips to Spokane and along the Montana Rail Link.

Thanks to John Gruber for numerous trips here and there, visits to Madison, Wisconsin, and for writing the sidebar about running modern AC diesels, and special thanks to Robert A. Buck of Tucker's Hobbies in Warren, Massachusetts, for trips, moral support, technical assistance, and publicity. Thanks, also, to Howard Ande, Don Gulbrandsen, Carl Swanson, F. L. Becht, Gerald Hook, Danny Johnson, Brian Rutherford, Vic Neves, David Monte Verde, Dean Sauvola, Mark Leppert, Norman Yellin, Tim Hensch, Marshall Beecher, Mike Schafer, Doug Moore, and Tessa Bold. Also, the Irish Railway Record Society, Milepost 92 1/2, the Colorado Railroad Museum, my father, and Tim Doherty all generously loaned me the use of their libraries.

I owe much of my knowledge of locomotives to fellow authors and locomotive enthusiasts. I grew up with a copy of Louis A. Marre and Jerry A. Pinkepank's original *Diesel Spotter's Guide*, and I've learned much from both writers over the years. In my capacity as editor at *Pacific RailNews*, I came to know Sean Graham-White and I've worked with him on several occasions. He is one of the most knowledgeable authors I know in the field of modern diesel locomotives. Over the years, Greg McDonnell, Paul Schneider, and J. David Ingles have published numerous informative articles on modern locomotives in the pages of *TRAINS* magazine. David Warner's features in *Passenger Train Journal* also stand out for their detailed coverage of modern passenger power. Jay Potter is another author whose exceptionally detailed writing elucidates the intricacies of modern diesel operation. Tim Zukas' self-published articles on locomotive performance helped me to better understand diesel-electrics. Books by John H. Armstrong, S. Kip Farrington, John R. Signor, Paul Withers of *Diesel Era*, Joseph Strapac, John Garmany, and others have all helped me track down, confirm, and comprehend facts, technical details, and locomotive minutia. The locomotive builders General Motors' Electro-Motive Division, General Electric, and Alco have produced enormous volumes of literature that have been extremely useful in understanding the technology, design, operation, and intended application of modern locomotives.

Thanks to the many professional railroaders who lent their experience, perspective, and knowledge to this work, including Steve Carlson, Craig Willett, Don Jilson, Ron Morales, Brian Burns, Thomas M. Hoover, Harry Vallas, Dick Gruber, and Robert Foreman. Special thanks, also, to Don Marson for his detailed explanations and photography.

Southern Pacific six-motor EMDs make music in the Tehachapis. Southern Pacific assigned its big six-motor EMDs indiscriminately, making little distinction between 3,000- and 3,600-horsepower units and routinely mixing tunnel and normal variations. An SD40 leads an SD40T-2, SD45, and another SD40T-2 at old Allard. *Photo by Brian Solomon*

Photography is an integral part of this book. In addition to my own photographs, I have included those of other photographers. They are duly credited for the images they made and/or supplied. Special thanks to Jim Shaughnessy, Mike Gardner, Tim Doherty, Tom Mangan, Dave Burton, George S. Pitarys, Brian Jennison, T. S. Hoover, Erik T. Hendrickson, Chris Burger, Patrick Yough, Tom Kline, and Doug Eisele.

Special thanks to my editor at MBI, Dennis Pernu, and to everyone else at MBI who assisted in the layout, design, and production of this book.

—Brian Solomon, Dublin 2002

INTRODUCTION

In the wake of World War II, diesel-electric locomotives rapidly vanquished steam power on American railways. This pioneering development of road diesels resulted in numerous cost savings desperately needed by railroads, which then faced ever-growing competition from highway and air transport. Although new diesel locomotives cost more than comparable steam designs and required a specialized labor force to maintain them, productivity gains afforded by the total switch to diesel power made for a wise investment. In the postwar market, four manufacturers competed for the bulk of new diesel sales.

The market leader was General Motors' Electro-Motive Division

(EMD), which had pioneered road diesel types during the 1930s and became the largest new locomotive builder after the war. The two largest steam locomotive builders, Alco and Baldwin, began selling diesel-electric locomotives in the 1930s. At first these companies focused on diesel switchers—then the largest and most lucrative diesel locomotive type—but following the war, both companies made serious efforts to sell road diesels as well. In the decade after the war, engine manufacturer Fairbanks-Morse also sold diesel locomotives. In just 15 years, from 1945 to 1960, American lines converted the bulk of their operations to diesel operation.

Electro-Motive SD45 demonstrators are seen at Cammal, Pennsylvania, on train BH-2. Cammal was a manual block station at the south end of Pine Creek Canyon on the New York Central Fallbrook Line between Lyons, New York, and Newberry Junction, Pennsylvania. Using a 20-cylinder 645 engine, EMD's SD45 was rated at 3,600 horsepower, making it one of the most powerful single-engine diesel-electric locomotives of its day. Today, locomotives are commonly rated at 4,000 horsepower and higher. *Chris Burger*

In the early 1960s, Alco made a last, but futile, attempt to compete in the domestic locomotive market by introducing its Century Series diesels. Its C-628 was a 2,750-horsepower six-motor model introduced in 1963. Although attractive, the Centuries didn't have what it took to keep Alco in the modern locomotive market, and in 1969 Alco ceased production at its Schenectady, New York, plant. However, its Canadian subsidiary continued to build locomotives in Montreal, and Bombardier eventually bought this line. A new Delaware & Hudson C-628 poses at Colonie, New York, in July 1965. *Jim Shaughnessy*

MK Rail was a locomotive contractor and remanufacturing company that attempted to enter the high-horsepower road locomotive business in the mid-1990s. An MK5000C in Southern Pacific paint is at MK Rail's Boise, Idaho, facility on September 27, 1994. *Don Marson*

Baldwin offered a six-motor diesel several years before Electro-Motive introduced its SD7. In the postwar period, six-motor diesels were considered specialty items and the concept didn't become popular with American railroads until the early 1960s. Trona Railway No. 54 is a Baldwin AS616 built in 1952. It was one of a handful of Baldwin road switchers that survived into the 1980s. Baldwin effectively exited the American market in the mid-1950s. *George S. Pitarys*

Opposite: Canadian Pacific has assembled a large fleet of AC traction diesels primarily comprised of General Electric AC4400CWs, such as these seen at Calgary, Alberta. By contrast, the other large Canadian system, Canadian National, has stuck with conventional DC traction diesels, ordering large numbers of modern six-motor types from both General Motors and General Electric. *Tim Doherty*

As steam disappeared, however, the market for new diesels began to diminish, resulting in poor sales, especially among the weaker builders—dieselization was complete, and the two weakest locomotive builders, Baldwin and Fairbanks-Morse, ended domestic production. Until the mid-1950s, Alco had built its diesel locomotives in conjunction with General Electric (GE), and its locomotives were identified as Alco-GE products. But General Electric split from Alco and began work on its own road diesel locomotive line (GE had been building electrics and small diesel switchers for years).

By 1956, GE was building road-diesels for export and in 1960 it switched its focus to the domestic market. The same year, Alco was selling just a fraction of GM's total, even though it was the second-largest locomotive manufacturer. But by mid-decade, GE had earned the number-two position and by the mid-1980s was the largest builder of new diesels. By contrast, Alco ultimately ended its domestic production in 1969, although its Canadian affiliate, Montreal Locomotive Works (MLW), continued for another decade to build Alco designs in small numbers.

In the late 1950s and 1960s, diesel builders set out to design better and more capable machines. Reliability and performance were improved upon in order to meet railroad demands. During this time the average output of single-unit locomotives was effectively doubled, while locomotives were at the same time made significantly more dependable and efficient.

For several reasons, the advent of the diesel had allowed railroads to markedly reduce the number of locomotives needed to move trains. Diesels required far less servicing than steam locomotives, they were more versatile, and, in most cases, more capable. Since diesels could be lashed up to work in multiple, a single engineer could haul much more tonnage with diesels than with steam. This ability, combined with superior tractive force and better braking power (afforded by the use of dynamic brakes) permitted railroads to operate significantly longer and heavier freight trains, allowing for a great labor savings. The diesel's ability to achieve maximum tractive effort from a start permitted the elimination of many helper districts where extra locomotives known as "helpers" were added to trains to assist over steeply

graded lines. Since diesels could also efficiently move heavy tonnage at greater speeds and required fewer serving stops (steam locomotives frequently needed to stop for coal and water), railroads, particularly in the West, were able to greatly speed up train schedules.

The basic advantages of diesel power inspired progressive railroads to push builders for even more powerful locomotives. In the late 1950s, following the example of Union Pacific, General Motors'

EMD boosted the output of its 567 engine by replacing its Roots blower with a turbocharger, resulting in the production of the 2,000-horsepower four-axle, four-motor GP20 and the 2,400-horsepower six-axle, six-motor SD24.

In the early days of commercial diesel production, most locomotives were four-motor machines. Passenger diesels, such as EMD's E-Units and Alco's PAs used six-axle, four-motor trucks in an A1A-A1A

The autumnal splendor of New England is a lush treat for visitors and residents alike. The passengers aboard Amtrak No. 448 (Boston section of the *Lake Shore Limited*) enjoy peak fall colors as their train descends through the Berkshires at Middlefield, Massachusetts, on the old Boston & Albany route. Leading the train is a single GE GENESIS P42 diesel. *Brian Solomon*

With its 20-cylinder engine drumming loudly, Santa Fe SD45 5366 leads an eastbound, upgrade toward the summit at Tehachapi, California. *Brian Solomon*

arrangement, where the center axle is not powered and used for better weight distribution. By the late 1940s, six-motor diesels were being built but were considered specialized machines. Indeed, when EMD introduced its first six-motor diesel, it was designated SD7, the "SD" standing for "Special Duty." Throughout the 1950s, four-motor locomotives dominated the market by a large margin, yet interest in six-motor diesels grew. By the mid-1960s, six-motor diesels had become

common, and by the later 1970s were more or less standard. Today, virtually every new freight diesel is a six-motor machine.

The early 1960s saw a significant leap forward in domestic diesel design. Electro-Motive's success with the GP20 led the company to introduce even more powerful turbocharged diesels: the 2,250-horsepower GP30 followed by the 2,500-horsepower GP35. The turbocharged GPs were in response to competition from Alco, General

Electric, and German diesel-hydraulic builder Krauss-Maffei, which had sold powerful machines to Southern Pacific and Denver & Rio Grande Western. Reliability issues, however, doomed the German hydraulics. But more powerful engines were only part of the story. Locomotive electrical systems were also improved, pressurized engine compartments introduced, and the low nose cab became a standard feature.

This book takes a look at "modern" high-powered diesel models from 1966 onward. Selected types producing 2,500 horsepower and greater are included. Since this is not intended as a comprehensive "spotting guide," no effort has been made to include examples of each and every type. Instead, 25 locomotive categories are highlighted in order to present greater depth than is possible in a typical guidebook. In addition to presenting locomotive statistics, these

Under cloudy skies, Santa Fe SD45 5324 climbs Ash Hill toward Barstow, California. *Brian Solomon*

sections describe market forces that motivated diesel development and railroad purchases, while giving real-life examples of locomotive application and performance. Railroads are as much about people and places as they are about machines, so in addition to locomotive statistics and performance analysis, there are stories and opinions from railroaders.

What makes a good locomotive? The criteria for judging a design vary greatly depending on individual outlook. Locomotive designers, railroad managers, locomotive engineers, and dyed-in-the-wool railroad enthusiasts may have greatly varied opinions on the virtues and drawbacks of different types. A locomotive designer, for example, wants a machine that will earn the best price and the most sales while furthering his or her company's reputation. Railroad managers, on the other hand, look at locomotives as tools for running a business and judge the machines by their overall cost effectiveness. Yet, each railroad has its own strategy for achieving this goal. Reliability, performance, and efficiency are all important in deciding the purchase and assignment of locomotives. An unreliable locomotive, no matter how powerful, is not as useful as a moderately powerful, reliable one. To the engineer who spends his day running the locomotive, ease of operation and comfort may be the most important considerations. Yet if the machine fails during the run and strands the engineer in the middle of nowhere, rest assured, he will be displeased. Casual enthusiasts may judge locomotives by more superficial criteria. A machine with a nice paint livery and a melodic horn may be more highly regarded than a drab-looking locomotive. Some enjoy listening to engines work, and a louder, throatier exhaust may add to the thrill. Others take a "team" approach and assign loyalties to a specific railroad or builder. There are numerous Alco-philes, for example, who have focused their interest on the pursuit of the last working Alco and MLW products, sometimes following them to the very ends of the earth.

Most locomotives today are built for heavy-haul freight service and are purchased for their ability to move trains cost-effectively rather than for their comfy seats or aesthetic attributes, although these latter criteria are sometimes taken into consideration. When a locomotive is described as "popular" in this book, it is strictly a measure of comparative sales and has no bearing on performance, the opinions of railroaders, or the feelings of enthusiasts. Electro-Motive's SD45–which, according to Jerry Pinkepank's *The Second Diesel Spotter's Guide*, sold 1,260 units–was a popular model. By contrast, General Electric's U25C, which sold just 113 units, was not popular.

This text includes many of the most common locomotives used on North American railroads today, as well as some of the more obscure types. A variety of different photographs have been selected to depict the machinery, but also to show locomotives working in scenic settings and to present a mood that conveys the spirit of modern railroading.

Opposite: Delaware & Hudson U30C 709 gets some work done at the railroad's Colonie, New York, shops. *Jim Shaughnessy*

Above: A railroader puts sand in an EMD SD45 demonstrator at Mechanicville, New York. Sand is spread on the rails to give added traction. *Jim Shaughnessy*

1 Electro-Motive SD40

Its magnificence was in its performance. Although not beautiful, the SD40 is among the best-liked locomotives among railroaders. Its 16-645 working hard, a Southern Pacific SD40 races eastward across the Utah Salt Flats. Brian Solomon

On the evening of March 6, 1997, an eastbound Union Pacific train on the former Southern Pacific line over Donner Pass grinds its way past Old Gorge, east of Alta, California. Leading the train is one of SP's 1960s-era SD40s. For more than 30 years Donner had been largely the domain of six-motor EMDs. *Brian Solomon*

The locomotive market in the mid-1960s was driven by the railroads' desire for locomotives sufficiently powerful to replace older models on a two-for-one basis (based on horsepower output). With its 2,500-horsepower four-motor GP35 and six-motor SD35 models of the early 1960s, Electro-Motive Division had reached the maximum practical output of its 567-engine design. Although 5,000 horsepower had been achieved in a single unit with the monster eight-axle, eight-motor DD35, this gigantic machine could only appeal to the likes of the large Western carriers.

Competition from General Electric, Alco, and German builder Krauss-Maffei prompted Electro-Motive to engineer an improved diesel engine and design a whole new line of more powerful and more reliable locomotives. EMD's successful 567 engine had been the powerplant in all of its road diesels since the late 1930s. This powerful and dependable two-cycle diesel engine was a sound design; all that was really required of a new engine was greater output. Electro-Motive essentially expanded the 567 engine by increasing the cylinder bore size, which resulted in increased displacement. The 567 engine was so named because each

cylinder has a 567-ci displacement. The new engine used a 9-1/16 inch cylinder bore and retained the 567's 10-inch stroke, which provided each cylinder with 645-ci displacement. Thus, the new engine was known as the 645 and manufactured in 6-, 8-, 12-, 16-, and 20-cylinder models. The smaller sizes were offered in both "normally aspirated" (using a Roots blower) and turbocharged models.

In 1964, EMD made exhaustive tests with experimental locomotives built using SD35 frames. Once it refined its new designs, it debuted a line of nine completely new models featuring the 645 engine, which entirely replaced the traditional 567 line. Of these new locomotive types, the high-horsepower models featured a completely new electrical transmission system, as well as a new prime mover. To harness the increased power of the turbocharged 645, EMD replaced the traditional generator with a state-of-the-art model AR-10 alternator and silicon diode rectifier. The AR-10 alternator produces variable frequency alternating current (AC) that is then rectified to direct current (DC) that powers the traction motors. (The AC/DC transmission system should not be confused with the development of three-phase AC

Conrail used pairs of old SD40s in helper service in the Alleghenies. Helpers were based at Cresson, Pennsylvania, a few miles past the summit on the west slope. Helpers shove westbound trains from Altoona up the mountain around the famous Horse Shoe Curve, but also work eastbound trains climbing to the summit from Johnstown, as well as coal branches. Conrail SD40 helpers are seen near "UN" in Gallitzin, Pennsylvania. *Brian Solomon*

traction that was applied in the early 1990s.) An alternator/solid-state rectifier combination is much more compact than a comparable generator, which was an important consideration because a generator capable of producing sufficient electrical power for the new high-output designs would have been excessively large. The AC/DC transmission also simplified maintenance because the alternator had fewer high-wear components. In addition, the alternator was not subject to "flashovers," a common flaw that plagued generators.

Greater electrical output also required a more substantial traction motor, so EMD's D67 gave way to the new D77 motor, which delivered more power and was more durable. In his book *Southern Pacific Dieselization*, John Garmany explains that the D77 derived its greater strength by using more copper in the armature coils and employing more durable synthetic insulation.

Electro-Motive announced its 645 models in 1965, and the first production locomotives featuring the new engine and electrical system were 50 GP40s rated at 3,000 horsepower and built for New York Central. On the heels of these four-motor machines were the 3,000-horsepower six-motor locomotives designated SD40s and the 3,600-horsepower SD45s. By the mid-1960s, railroads were routinely operating longer and heavier trains that made these new powerful six-motor locomotives far more popular than comparable models of a decade earlier. Railroads bought the SD40s by the hundreds and the model remained in production until 1972, when EMD introduced its

even more successful SD40-2. Without question, the SD40 was one of the most successful locomotive designs of the 1960s. They were well liked by railroads and railroaders alike, and many an engineer will tell you that the only locomotive he likes better than an SD40 is an SD40-2!

The durability of the SD40 has allowed some to remain in heavy service for more than three decades, in some cases serving three or four owners. New England Central, which operates the former Central Vermont Railway between St. Albans, Vermont, and New London, Connecticut, has used two former Conrail SD40s that were originally owned by Penn-Central. Despite their age, and still wearing faded Conrail-blue paint, these locomotives were regularly assigned to New England Central's heaviest freights and were well liked by crews. Steve Carlson, a former New England Central engineer, often ran New England Central's nightly freight from Brattleboro, Vermont, to Palmer, Massachusetts. This is a heavy train that forwards traffic from Canadian National (CN) and Vermont Rail System to customers in southern New England, and typically moves paper and timber products, as well as other heavy materials such as cement, coal, and copper.

When asked about the old SD40s, Carlson laughs and says, "They are one of the nicest engines I've ever run."

Carlson notes that on a typical night the southbound freight would be hauled by a pair of SD40s and two GP38s with 80 to 100 cars in tow. Such a train would weigh between 8,000 and 9,000 tons, making it one of the heaviest mixed freights in New England. South

A former Conrail SD40 leads northbound New England Central freight No. 323 across the White River at West Hartford, Vermont. New England Central often assigns hand-me-down SD40s to its freights between Palmer, Massachusetts, and St. Albans, Vermont. *Brian Solomon*

of Brattleboro, the New England Central follows an undulating profile that Carlson describes as a "roller coaster." To illustrate his point, he explains, "There are places where a 100-car train will be winding through three sets of curves and stretched across three undulations."

From an engineer's perspective this can be the most challenging type of operation. Unlike a continuous upgrade where the engineer can just leave the locomotives in "Run 8" (highest throttle position), an undulating profile requires constant attention to keep the train moving properly. By using throttle modulation, the engineer keeps the train stretched and prevents the slack from running in. Rough train handling can easily result in damaged merchandise. If the slack runs in particularly hard, it can cause a broken drawbar or coupler.

Carlson continues, "It's all a matter of judging your speed and knowing where you are." Using a technique called "balancing the grade," the engineer keeps the train at track speed by throttling up and throttling back as needed. "When cresting a grade, you reduce speed slowly, notching back the throttle to keep the train from slamming into you as it comes over the top," Carlson explains.

South of Amherst, Massachusetts, the railroad begins its 6-mile assault of Belchertown Hill. This is no Donner Pass, and its ruling grade is in the vicinity of only 1.3 percent, yet it's a tough pull and the sustained gradient can easily stall an underpowered train. "There's a short grade at Miller's Falls [north of Amherst]," Carlson recalls, "where the line climbs over the Boston & Maine. While it isn't much of a hill, this

[little grade] would be your first indication after leaving Brattleboro whether or not you would have a chance on Belchertown [Hill]." Bringing a heavy train south over Belchertown, Carlson would keep his eye on the speed of the train and on the ampmeter. Normally, a train would drop to about 10 miles per hour while climbing the grade. However, if it dropped much below 10 and the ampmeter was running in the red, there was a chance he might stall and have to double the hill (take the train up in two sections, one at a time).

Carlson notes that under a normal load, the ampmeter, which measures current to the traction motors, would read in the 400- to 600-amp range. As the locomotives start to dig into the grade, however, more power is needed. If the motors start to draw in the 1,200-amp range, the meter is in the "red zone" and, based on short-time ratings, the traction motors can only operate for about 10 minutes without risking damage. At 1,400 amps, about five minutes is the limit. "At some point the train will slow to the point where the wheels will just start spinning," Carlson says. By the time that happens, "the show is over," and there's no choice but to double the hill. Hearing a heavy train stall on the grade is a real experience in itself, as it demonstrates maximum locomotive performance and results in lots of noise and sand.

The day of the traditional SD40 has nearly come to a close. Soon, more modern machines will supersede the need to maintain such antique machines. But when they are all gone, operating men, as well as locomotive enthusiasts, will miss them.

2 General Electric U30C

Southern Pacific was among General Electric's best customers for its early road locomotives. SP owned 68 of GE's pioneering U25Bs, three of the eight-motor U50Cs, and later purchased a sizeable fleet of six-motor GEs, including 37 U30Cs and 88 U33Cs. SP tended to use its GE six-motors on its graded lines in southern California. On March 30, 1970, five SP U33Cs lead a freight at Hiland at the summit of Cajon Pass. Brian Jennison

Delaware & Hudson U30C No. 707 at the railroad's Colonie, New York, shops in May 1968. Delaware & Hudson bought most of its new locomotives from Alco and General Electric. Its attractive "Lightning Stripe" livery was popular with railroad enthusiasts. *Jim Shaughnessy*

Opposite: New Delaware & Hudson U30Cs are seen at Mechanicville, New York, in 1967. The D&H had just 12 U30Cs. In 1979, they were sold for service in Mexico. *Jim Shaughnessy*

General Electric was a well-established locomotive manufacturer when it introduced its domestic Universal road diesel line in 1960. By that time, GE had been building locomotives and supplying locomotive components for more than 60 years. While the other diesel manufacturers—Electro-Motive, Fairbanks-Morse, and the steam-turned-diesel builders Alco and Baldwin—dominated the locomotive supply scene in the immediate postwar period, General Electric had also played a significant role in locomotive and locomotive component development. Its most prominent position was as Alco's electrical partner in Alco's early diesel years. General Electric and Alco had worked together as early as 1925 on joint diesel projects, and Alco's diesels carried joint Alco-GE builder's plates until the early 1950s when the arrangement dissolved.

Under its own name, General Electric had produced a host of locomotive designs, including straight-electrics, steam turbines, and gas-electrics, as well as a wide variety of small diesel-electrics for switching and branchline service. Less obvious was GE's design and supply of locomotive electrical components. According to an article in the November 1966 *TRAINS* magazine, one of GE's greatest strengths was in its motor design. Its 752 Series traction motor was used in thousands of postwar locomotives, including the entire Alco line. In addition, EMD's traction motors today are largely derived from GE designs.

Following its break with Alco, GE set about developing its own road locomotive line. The task was not accomplished overnight, but took several years. It built test locomotives and demonstrators, then, starting about 1956, entered the road locomotive export market. By the time GE finally introduced its domestic Universal locomotive, the 2,500-horsepower U25B, for sale in 1960, it had obtained considerable experience with its product.

Today, there is virtually no market for a road locomotive with a mere 2,500 horsepower. Machines with 4,000 horsepower are considered standard, and both GE and EMD offer 6,000-horsepower locomotives. But when the U25B was new, it was the most powerful diesel-electric locomotive available. By comparison, EMD's most powerful four-axle was its 2,000-horsepower GP20, and its most powerful six-axle was the 2,400-horsepower SD24. At that time, because railroads were beginning to seek significantly greater power in single-unit locomotives, GE focused its effort on the high-horsepower freight market.

The success of GE's new U25B has been well documented. According to Louis A. Marre's *Diesel Locomotives: The First 50 Years*, GE built 476 U25Bs between 1959 and 1966. Although this was small compared to EMD's high-horsepower four-motor sales during the same period, the U25B and its kin allowed General Electric to establish itself in the road locomotive market, taking second place in sales behind EMD and surpassing longtime builder Alco.

During the 1960s, locomotive builders gradually upped locomotive output. By 1966, all three builders offered locomotives with 3,000-horsepower-and-higher output. In this same period, six-motor designs, which had been considered specialized machines, were accepted as standard road locomotives by many large railroads. Improved reliability of six-motor diesels combined with their greater tractive effort made them especially appealing to lines with heavy grades. Southern Pacific, Great Northern, Pennsylvania, Santa Fe, and Union Pacific, to name a few, all purchased large numbers of six-motor diesels for general road service. General Electric's six-motor U25C had not enjoyed the same widespread popularity of the U25B: Marre's totals indicate that just 113 were built between 1963 and 1965.

General Electric improved its product line to match trends in the market. In addition to boosting output, first to 2,800 horsepower with the U28B and U28C, then with the introduction of 3,000- and 3,300-horsepower models, GE also introduced the pressurized engine compartment and AC/DC electric transmission system along the lines of those introduced by Alco and EMD (see the SD40 section). The demand for six-motor diesels, combined with increased horsepower and GE's improved quality, resulted in General Electric selling many six-motor diesels in the late 1960s and early 1970s. Its most popular model was the 3,000-horsepower U30C (of which Marre indicates 592 were sold in a nine-year period starting in 1967) and the U33C, which

sold 375 from 1968 to 1975. In addition, GE also built a U36C model that sold 124 units domestically beginning in 1971. The variations in horsepower allowed railroads to tailor their locomotive purchases based on maximum output.

In 1976, GE discontinued its Universal line with the debut of its new and improved DASH 7 line. By this time only EMD and GE remained in the American domestic market, Alco having exited in 1969, and its Canadian subsidiary, MLW, playing only a minor role in new locomotive production.

Above: Burlington Northern assigned many of its six-motor GEs to heavy coal service. This U30C was based at Alliance, Nebraska. *Brian Solomon*

Opposite: Three Delaware & Hudson U30Cs grind up Richmondville Hill on their way to Binghamton, New York, from Mechanicville. The Delaware & Hudson was an anthracite coal hauler that evolved into a bridge line. Today, the D&H route is operated by Canadian Pacific. *Jim Shaughnessy*

3 Electro-Motive SD45

The first production SD45 was Great Northern No. 400, named "Hustle Muscle" to show off the locomotive's power and speed potential. Today, this historic machine is preserved on the North Shore Scenic at Duluth, Minnesota. Brian Solomon

The SD45 conveys power; its Spartan yet brawny appearance says it means business, while its deafening roar working in Run 8 lets you know you are dealing with a serious and powerful locomotive. Imagine the still silence of the Nevada desert at twilight; unlike so much of the modern world, there are few sounds here, perhaps just a gentle wind and the distant buzz of an airplane. The railroad is quiet, the signals dark. Nothing has passed in hours. Then, off to the west, beyond your line of sight, you can hear the pulsing, low

bass of SD45s hauling a heavy eastbound. When three or more work in tandem, there is no other sound like it. If the wind is right, you might even be able to hear SD45s working more than 15 miles away. *This* is the unintended beauty of EMD's 20-cylinder 645E3 engine, the power behind the 3,600-horsepower SD45.

Like Electro-Motive's SD40, the SD45 model was introduced in 1965 and, following extensive testing, production began in 1966. Apart from its larger engine, the SD45 employed much of the same

The "flared" radiators on its long hood characterize the SD45 body. On March 29, 1992, a Southern Pacific SD45 running long hood–first leads a helper set downgrade near Marcel in the Tehachapi Mountains of California. *Brian Solomon*

equipment as the SD40: it used the same platform, AR-10 alternator, and D-77 traction motors. From the front, the SD45 shared the appearance of most contemporary EMD road locomotives. However, the back of the locomotive was exemplified by tapered angular radiators designed to allow for the greater airflow needed because of the higher output. The attraction of the SD45 was high tractive effort and high horsepower, the key ingredients for power and speed. Yet, unlike earlier high-horsepower machines that employed dual engines, the

SD45 used just a single engine. John Garmany indicates in *Southern Pacific Dieselization* that Southern Pacific (SP) embraced the SD45 rather than endure further trials with dual-engine locomotives like EMD's DD35, which it had experimented with in the early 1960s.

Many lines, particularly in the West, viewed this new machine as the solution to their power needs. The Great Northern received the first SD45, which it dubbed "Hustle Muscle." The Southern Pacific, Santa Fe, and Burlington Northern (formed through the merger of Burlington,

Great Northern, Northern Pacific, and Spokane, Portland & Seattle) had some of the largest fleets. The type was no stranger in the East, either—as the Pennsylvania Railroad and Erie-Lackawanna took interest in the type, other lines like the Reading also sampled the 20-cylinder monsters. In addition, Midwestern lines such as Chicago & North Western (C&NW) and the Milwaukee Road, and the Southern lines Norfolk & Western (N&W), Atlantic Coast Line, and Southern Railway acquired SD45s. Garmany indicates that a new SD45 cost about $290,000 at the time, although the actual cost depended on the options ordered from EMD and the size of the order.

According to Louis A. Marre and Jerry Pinkepank's *The Contemporary Diesel Spotter's Guide*, 1,260 SD45s were sold over the locomotive's lifetime. Yet the locomotive is known to have suffered from some mechanical troubles. Early on, there were numerous complaints of broken crankshafts, a malady that has been attributed in part to the great power of the engine combined with the unusual length of the shaft

March 23, 1989, dawned bright and clear as an eastbound Delaware & Hudson train was working its way east from Buffalo, New York. At the time, New York, Susquehanna & Western (NYSW) was the designated operator for D&H. An NYSW SD45 leads the train at Alden, New York. Things were not running smoothly this day: a little while later, the train stalled climbing Attica Hill. *Brian Solomon*

The SD70MAC is Burlington Northern Santa Fe's choice for Powder River coal service. Since 1994, the railroad has acquired hundreds of these powerful AC traction machines. *Tim Doherty and Tom Mangan*

With more than three decades of hard service behind them, these Wisconsin Central SD45s are running on borrowed time. In 2001, Canadian National took control of WC, and it's just a matter of time before the SD45s are stricken from active service. But on February 6, 2002, a pair of SD45s was seen lifting a heavy train up Byron Hill, south of Fond du Lac, Wisconsin. *Brian Solomon*

needed for 20 cylinders. (EMD's 16-cylinder engine didn't suffer from the same problem, and has a better reputation.) The SD45's reputation has been clouded by the crankshaft problem for more than th decades, despite the fact that the difficulty seems to have been ov come. However, greater maintenance costs and significantly high fuel consumption made the SD45 unpopular with some railroad: Other problems included leaky radiators and inequitable weight dis tribution, which could result in a harmonic rocking at moderate speeds on poor track. Don Jilson, a locomotive engineer for Conrail, explains, "The SD45 would develop a severe harmonic at about 15 to

18 miles per hour. The locomotives would start to bounce at that speed, and one time I broke a rail on the old [New York] Central mainline near Syracuse. Of course, we still had the old jointed rails."

During the recession in the early 1980s, some roads purged SD45s from their rosters, favoring SD40s and newer SD40-2s that were cheaper to operate. Milwaukee Road had just a dozen SD45s, along with its five FP45s (which also use the 20-cylinder 645). Craig Willett, a former Milwaukee Road engineer, explains that when the railroad scaled back its operations following tough times in the 1970s, it decided to focus on its most common locomotive types and dispose of most of its

Three Wisconsin Central SD45s lead a southbound freight at Byron, Wisconsin, on June 30, 1996. *Brian Solomon*

Always looking for a motive power bargain, Guilford acquired former Norfolk Southern high-hood SD45s for its Springfield Terminal subsidiary in 1987. East of Mechanicville, New York, on August 19, 1988, Guilford SD45 682 leads a coal train destined for Bow, New Hampshire. *Brian Solomon*

On March 8, 1977, a pair of Union Pacific SD45s leads three other EMDs, including an SP SD40 at Dale Junction, Wyoming, on Sherman Hill. The SD45 did not last as long on the UP as 16-cylinder EMD models from the same period. *James P. Marcus, Doug Eisele collection*

Opposite: The Delaware & Hudson operated just the three SD45s seen here on Halloween 1968 crossing the Mohawk River Bridge in Schenectady, New York. Delaware & Hudson preferred GE and Alco products, and in 1969 D&H exchanged these orphan EMDs for three Erie Lackawanna U33Cs. *Jim Shaughnessy*

"odd ball" locomotives, including its 20-cylinder EMDs. About the same time, Conrail and Union Pacific also shed their SD45 fleets.

Still, other railroads received very good service from their SD45s. Southern Pacific and Santa Fe rebuilt their SD45 fleets, which prolonged their service lives past the 30-year mark. Some SD45 rebuilding jobs have addressed difficulties with the 20-cylinder engine either by de-rating or replacement. MK Rail in Boise, Idaho, has remanufactured many SD45s, installing 16-cylinder 645s in place of the 20-cylinder versions. This reduces the output of the locomotive to just 3,000 horsepower, effectively making it an SD40. MK Rail, which also installed modern microprocessor electronics on its later rebuilds, designates its rebuilds as "SD40-3s," the "-3" indicating the microprocessor, the trademark of the diesel-electric's so-called "third generation."

Surplus SD45s shunned by the larger railroads such as Burlington Northern, found new owners in the 1980s. Regional lines such as New York, Susquehanna & Western, Montana Rail Link, and Guilford bought up these big EMD's at bargain prices and put them to work in mainline service. Regional start-up Wisconsin Central assembled one of the largest fleets of secondhand 20-cylinder locomotives, acquiring more than 100 SD45s, F45s, and other 20-cylinder models, many of which the railroad rebuilt at its shops in North Fond du Lac, Wisconsin. Wisconsin Central operated portions of the old Soo Line and Chicago & North Western, as well as bits of Green Bay & Western, from northern Illinois, across Wisconsin to Michigan's Upper Peninsula and into eastern Minnesota. Under the direction of

Ed Burkhardt, Wisconsin Central (WC) built up a robust freight business that became the talk of the industry. Burkhardt's unconventional strategies, aggressive pursuit of new business, and desire to provide customers with good service won WC a large share of new traffic. By the mid-1990s, WC was running as many as 15 round trips daily on its mainline between its yards at North Fond du Lac and Chicago. It operated freight trains on a scheduled basis and kept train lengths within manageable proportions.

The SD45 was highly regarded by Wisconsin Central and was the mainstay of the railroad's road fleet, being favored over more common 16-cylinder models. WC put a lot of work into its used locomotives, overhauling them to a like-new condition. The attraction of the SD45 was simple: by the mid-1980s, a secondhand SD45 cost significantly less than an SD40 of the same age because of the SD45's higher fuel and maintenance costs. Initially, WC solved the SD45's fuel consumption issues with a nominal engine de-rating. Don Marson, an experienced railroader who worked for Wisconsin Central in the mid-1990s, explains that WC restored the 3,600-horsepower rating to its SD45s when the units were sent in for major overhaul. The railroad renumbered the modified SD45s from the 6500/6600 Series to the 7500 Series to reflect this upgrade. Wisconsin Central also equipped its SD45s with Q-Tron, an aftermarket computer system manufactured in Canada and designed to enhance adhesion by 20 percent though superior wheel-slip management.

Wisconsin Central's SD45s performed well and were routinely assigned to freights in sets of two or three units. On the busy Fond du Lac–to–Chicago line, southbound WC trains faced Byron Hill immediately south of the city of Fond du Lac. This grade, about a 5-mile, 1 percent climb, is the most difficult operating challenge on the run to Chicago and would routinely cause heavy trains to drop to a crawl. According to Marson, two of WC's Q-Tron SD45s could singly lift 7,200 tons over Byron Hill at a speed of 11 to 12 miles per hour. Wisconsin Central also operated especially heavy ore trains over Byron. To avoid assigning four or five locomotives all the way to Chicago, WC would assign just three SD45s to the head end, with a two-unit helper to lift the heavy trains over Byron Hill. The 20-cylinder roar of SD45s fore and aft on a loaded taconite run was a typical sound on Byron in the mid-1990s. In 2001, Canadian National absorbed the Wisconsin Central. As of this writing in 2002, many SD45s remain active on old WC lines, but their days are numbered.

Although examples of SD45s remain in service, the heyday of the 20-cylinder 645 has come and gone. Several SD45s have been preserved. Great Northern's original "Hustle Muscle" has been restored to its original livery and operates on the North Shore Scenic Railway based in Duluth, Minnesota. According to *The Semaphore* newsletter edited by David Clinton, Union Pacific has donated Southern Pacific's first SD45, originally numbered 8800, to the Utah State Railroad Museum.

4 Electro-Motive DDA40X

Electro-Motive's DDA40X, built exclusively for Union Pacific, was the largest and most powerful single-unit diesel locomotive ever constructed. UP received 47 of them between 1969 and 1971. This one is preserved at the Portola Railroad Museum in Portola, California. Most DDA40Xs were out of service by 1984. Brian Solomon

Union Pacific desired more powerful single-unit locomotives in order to use fewer units on heavy trains. Fifteen DD35As were built for UP in 1964 and 1965 to supplement cabless DD35s (sometimes classified DD35Bs). By March 31, 1979, these DD35s were reaching the end of their service lives when they were photographed at Barstow, California. *Brian Jennison*

Union Pacific's (UP) historic transcontinental routes move massive quantities of freight over long distances. To move that freight economically, UP has historically run very long and heavy trains requiring lots of motive power. In the steam era, Union Pacific had some of the largest locomotives ever built. Big steam reduced the need for double-heading and so saved crew costs. UP's three-cylinder 4-12-2 Union Pacific types—the largest non-articulated steam locomotives in North America—were commonly used on its flatland run across Nebraska from Omaha to North Platte. Later, with Alco's help, UP developed the high-speed articulated 4-6-6-4 "Challenger" for moving freight and passengers on more sinuous lines. But UP's ultimate steam locomotives were its well-known 4-8-8-4 "Big Boys," designed to lift very heavy "fruit blocks," priority perishable trains carrying California produce over the Wasatch Range and eastward from Ogden, Utah, to Green River and Cheyenne, Wyoming. A Big Boy could generate more horsepower than even the most modern diesels can today.

UP's quest for big power wasn't relegated to traditional reciprocating steam. In the late 1930s, Union Pacific tested an enormously powerful General Electric steam turbine. In the 1950s, the railroad assembled the only large fleet of gas-turbine locomotives, which were among the most powerful internal-combustion locomotives ever built and rated at 8,500 horsepower. In the mid- to late 1950s, Union Pacific followed a more common path, and bought a large number of EMD four-motor diesels, but needed to lash up large numbers of them to

haul freight. By the early 1960s new, more powerful diesels were developed that allowed for unit reduction on heavy trains. At this time, Union Pacific expressed interest in "double-diesels" for freight service, which would allow for even greater unit reduction and, in theory, greater savings.

Although the double-diesel concept may seem awkward and cumbersome today, at that time it was commonplace. Electro-Motive developed its double-diesel E-Unit in the mid-1930s for passenger service and the type was widely used all over America. Also, both Baldwin and Lima Hamilton had sold double-engine "transfer diesels" in the late 1940s and early 1950s. To meet Union Pacific's needs, all three American diesel manufacturers built very high-horsepower diesel road switchers with dual prime movers and eight axles. EMD announced its DD35 first, but General Electric's U50 was the first of the new double-diesels that was ready to go. Alco built a single set of C855s in an A-B-A configuration (the center unit was a cabless "booster"). EMD's 5,000-horsepower DD35 was conceived as a cabless booster that was essentially two 2,500-horsepower GP35s under one frame and was envisioned to run in an A-B-A arrangement with GP35s. The DD35 rode on four-axle Flexicoil trucks, which provided the "DD" designation. (A two-axle truck is a "B," a three-axle is a "C," and, logically, a four-axle is a "D.") However, "DD" can just as easily mean "double-diesel," so the designation works well from two perspectives. General Electric's U50s used four two-axle trucks in a B-B+B-B wheel arrangement adapted for the gas-turbine designs.

The rationale for a cabless design was consistent with the desire for lower costs through unit reduction. Cabs cost money, and reducing the number of locomotives with cabs in a large consist potentially results in lower per-unit costs. However, the lack of a cab sacrifices flexibility. Later, EMD built DD35As that featured driver cabs. Only Union Pacific and Southern Pacific bought double-diesels, with UP acquiring the bulk of them. The introduction of new high-horsepower six-motor models in the mid-1960s satisfied SP's motive power needs, and it didn't pursue more double-diesel designs. When EMD debuted its new line of 645 diesels in 1965 and 1966, it included a DD40 model, which would have been a 6,000-horsepower machine powered by a pair of 16-cylinder 645 engines—essentially a double GP40—but the model was never actually built.

In 1969, Union Pacific took renewed interest in double-diesels and ordered new models from both General Electric and EMD. General Electric built its U50C, a 5,000-horsepower model that featured a C-C wheel arrangement, while EMD produced its DDA40X, the largest and most powerful commercial diesel locomotive ever built. The DDA40X was a unique design with several distinctive attributes, including its great size. It was a full 10 feet longer than the DD35, measuring 98 feet, 5 inches. (This is also 18 feet longer than the modern SD80MAC and SD90MAC.) A pair of 16-cylinder 645E3 diesels powers the DDA40X, and can generate a 6,600-horsepower maximum output. Compared to the 3,000-horsepower SD40, which used the same engine, each 16-cylinder 645E3 engine in the

DDA40X produced 300 additional horsepower in the highest throttle position. This was achieved by increasing the maximum engine rpm.

Another distinctive feature was the cowl-style cab that used a full-width nose and large two-piece windshield. The design predated the now-common North American Safety Cab by two decades, although the cowl cab set design precedents that would later influence the Safety Cab. Not to be forgotten was the DDA40X's modern, simplified electrical system that used solid-state modules that could be quickly replaced in the advent of failure. A variant of this electrical system became a standard feature on EMD's DASH 2 line beginning in 1972. Since 1969 was the one hundredth anniversary of the completion of the first Transcontinental Railroad—completed on May 10, 1869, with the famous Golden Spike Ceremony at Promontory, Utah—the DDA40Xs were numbered the 6900 Series and became known as "Centennials." The class locomotive, number 6900, was even used to haul a commemorative "special" around the system.

The eight-axle diesels had a fairly short tenure. The Centennials probably had the longest and most productive service lives, but most only lasted in regular service for little more than a decade. Although they were stored during the economic recession in the early 1980s, many were revived in 1984 when traffic started to pick up. Several Union Pacific DDA40Xs have been preserved, and one locomotive, number 6936, is retained by UP for its Historic Fleet, where it is used for excursions and publicity, but has occasionally been pressed into regular freight service when traffic demands.

Above: Union Pacific routinely assigned its big double-diesels to its Los Angeles & Salt Lake Route. On January 31, 1976, a pair of DDA40Xs and an SD26B leads a train at Sullivan's Curve in Cajon Pass, California. *Brian Jennison*

Below: This head-on view was made of Union Pacific DDA40X 6930 at the Illinois Railway Museum at Union, Illinois. Union Pacific has been very generous in preserving their historic equipment. *Brian Solomon*

5 Electro-Motive FP45

The FP45 was developed by EMD for Santa Fe passenger service. The cowl design was later adapted for the freight-service F45 and other locomotives. Santa Fe FP45 is seen at Woodford, California, in January 1991. Brian Solomon

On April 7, 1991, a pair of former Burlington Northern F45s leads the westbound Transcisco Tour Train at Shed 10 on Donner Pass. This private luxury tour train operated between San Jose, California, and Reno, Nevada. Trancisco's three F45s later went to Wisconsin Southern and then to Montana Rail Link. *Brian Solomon*

In the early days of commercial diesel production, aesthetics mattered. During the 1930s and 1940s, streamlining was all the rage with industrial designers, and "streamlined" was synonymous with "modern." In order to put road diesels in the best light and ensure their popularity, every effort was made to make them look good. Streamlining and fancy paint schemes were the order of the day. Electro-Motive's E-Units and F-Units (as well as similar models by Alco, Baldwin, and Fairbanks-Morse) used streamlined "car body" designs, in which the outer shell was integral to the locomotive's structure, not just decorative shrouding. Once the railroads had been sold on dieselization and steam was on its way out, however, new road diesel designs took on a more utilitarian appearance. The GP9 prevailed over the F9 in sales by a large margin. The last traditional F-Units sold in the United States were dual-mode passenger-only FL9s for the New Haven in 1960.

Although the road switcher type had its cost advantages, there was still a market for a covered locomotive. In the mid-1960s, Santa Fe expressed a desire for new shrouded diesels, initially for its long-distance passenger trains and premier freight services. Both Electro-Motive and General Electric adapted modern designs with shrouding to meet Santa

Fe's request, and in 1968 EMD built nine FP45s for Santa Fe. The locomotive was basically a covered version of the SD45 with a large steam generator for passenger service (in the 1960s, American passenger trains still used steam for train heat, a carryover from steam locomotives).

Although not streamlined in the style of the E- and F-Units, the FP45 featured a cleaner overall appearance than did contemporary road switchers. While the front end had used a wide-cab design and cleaner lines than the typical EMDs of the period, the rest of the locomotive was covered in angular boxlike shrouds known as "cowls" (in fact, locomotives so covered are sometimes called cowls). The cowl shrouding has practical advantages as well as aesthetic ones. It reduces wind resistance, which is important when moving at high speeds, which the Santa Fe did—it operated its passenger trains on fast schedules and was one of the last railroads in the United States to maintain a 90-mile-per-hour mainline. In addition, the shrouds protect crewmembers when walking from locomotive to locomotive while traveling at speed, and makes running maintenance safer and easier than on road switchers where crews would be exposed. Also, unlike

In the mid-1990s, Wisconsin Central augmented its fleet of SD45s with several former Santa Fe F45s and a single FP45. On March 22, 1996, a Wisconsin Central F45 leads a Chicago-bound freight through Waukesha, Wisconsin. *Brian Solomon*

In the early 1980s, Santa Fe substantially rebuilt its F45s and changed their railroad designation to "SDF45." One of these rebuilt locomotives is seen leading a freight at Becker, New Mexico, on December 10, 1985. *Don Marson*

those on E- and F-Units, the FP45 cowl shrouds were not part of the locomotive structure.

Santa Fe's FP45s were painted in its attractive red-and-silver "war bonnet" scheme used for passenger locomotives. In their early days, they were often assigned to Santa Fe's finest passenger trains, including the deluxe Chicago–Los Angeles *Super Chief*. But Santa Fe's FP45 was intended as a dual-service machine and also used in fast

freight service. The only other customer for the FP45 was the Milwaukee Road, which had just five of them.

EMD also built a freight cowl along the lines of the FP45, but which lacked the large steam generator and was designated an F45. Santa Fe ordered 40 F45s, along with Great Northern and its successor, Burlington Northern, which bought 56. Like the SD45, both the FP45 and F45 were rated at 3,600 horsepower and used EMD's 20-cylinder

645E3 engine. EMD went on to develop the cowl design for passenger services, building both four- and six-motor models with 16-cylinder 645 engines. The most popular of these locomotives was the F40PH that became Amtrak's standard power for the better part of two decades from the mid-1970s onward.

Santa Fe's and Milwaukee's FP45s were used in freight service in the 1970s after Amtrak assumed operation of long-distance passenger services in 1971. Santa Fe had a tradition of running fast freight and often assigned its cowl locomotives to its "Super-C" Chicago–Los Angeles intermodal run. In 1989, under the direction of Michael Haverty, Santa Fe made a splash by reintroducing its war bonnet paint, first repainting its FP45 fleet for its Super Fleet road intermodal services. From that point on, all new Santa Fe road locomotives were delivered in the war bonnet livery. Early on, Milwaukee Road assigned its 20-cylinder locomotives, including its FP45s, to its Pacific Extension, but in later years reassigned them to work on its St. Paul–Kansas City

and St. Paul–Chicago mainlines. Milwaukee's 20-cylinder locomotives had much shorter careers than Santa Fe's, and were withdrawn from service in the early 1980s. According to engineer Craig Willett, the railroad tried to keep its 20-cylinder locomotives together. Of running the FP45s, Willett said, "They were all right if you could keep them running, but they were rough-riding engines. If you had them on bad track, it was like being at sea!" Other engineers have echoed this complaint.

Like the more common SD45, cowl 20-cylinder locomotives found new work in lease fleets and on regional railroads in the 1980s and early 1990s. New York, Susquehanna & Western, Wisconsin Central, Wisconsin Southern, and Montana Rail Link all variously operated F45s. Wisconsin Central also operated a former Santa Fe FP45. For a very brief period beginning in December 1990, a privately operated luxury excursion train called the Transcisco Tour Train, used three former Burlington Northern F45s on its San Jose, California–Reno, Nevada, run over Southern Pacific's Donner Pass.

Below left: The sun sets through the reeds in the shadow of a former Santa Fe F45 on Wisconsin Central. *Brian Solomon*

Below right: Cab detail of Wisconsin Central F45 No. 6656. *Brian Solomon*

6 Electro-Motive SD40-2

Burlington Northern's vast fleet of more than 800 SD40-2s were among the most common sights in Western railroading for more than a decade. Here, three BN SD40-2s lead a BNSF eastbound intermodal train at Steward, Illinois, on the evening of June 24, 1996. Brian Solomon

Three SD40-2s and a General Electric C30-7 lift a Union Pacific westbound up Encina Hill near Oxman, Oregon, on June 12, 1993. The series of three successive summits in eastern Oregon pose a serious challenge to Union Pacific operations on the route from Granger, Wyoming, to Portland, Oregon. *Brian Solomon*

Introduced in 1972, Electro-Motive's DASH 2 line was all about making good things better. EMD's 645-engine locomotives were already well liked for their performance and dependability. They were the bestselling machines on the market and nearly every major railroad in North America was using them in large numbers. DASH 2 models were in essence improved variations of the models that preceded them. For example, a GP40-2 used the same basic components as the GP40. Horsepower output was the same, and in the case of the GP40-2, there were very few external modifications. In an earlier era, EMD may have marked such changes to its line by introducing a whole new number series, in the way it had upgraded the F3 to the F7. By simply adding a

"-2" after existing model designations, EMD preserved its basic nomenclature while highlighting a host of improvements to its line.

The most significant innovation of the DASH 2 line was its entirely revamped electrical system. Modular solid-state electronics were introduced to simplify the electrical control system. Replacing traditional electrical circuits and relays dramatically reduced the number of electrical components, improved reliability, and eased maintenance. In the event of component failure, modular cards could be easily exchanged, making locomotive repair quick and easy.

The SD40 and SD40-2 are often grouped together because the models seem so similar; the subtleties of electrical component changes are invisible to most observers. However, the SD40-2 featured a number of other changes that made it a different and noticeably better locomotive than the SD40.

From a performance perspective one of the most important attributes of the SD40-2 was the introduction of EMD's new HTC truck (sometimes spelled HT-C). This redesigned three-motor truck replaced the standard three-motor Flexicoil truck used on most EMD six-motor locomotives. According to John Garmany in *Southern Pacific Dieselization*, the HTC truck was first used by EMD on its 4,200-horsepower SD40X demonstrators.

The truck's designation stands for "high-traction," with "C" indicating three motors. Similar in appearance to the Flexicoil truck, the HTC used an improved motor arrangement, better dampening, and other innovations to achieve a more effective weight transfer and thus permit better wheel-to-rail adhesion. Externally, the HTC truck is most easily identified by the presence of a dampener on the second axle that resembles an automotive shock absorber. Based on data in Sean Graham-White's article, "Power for the Future," in *Extra 2200 South*, Issue 110, the continuous adhesion factor was boosted from 18 percent on the SD40 to 21 percent on the SD40-2.

In ideal conditions, the SD40-2 is given a 27 percent adhesion rating. The SD40-2 is slightly longer too. According to Louis A. Marre and Paul K. Withers' *The Contemporary Diesel Spotter's Guide, 2000 Edition*, the SD40-2 rides on a 68-foot, 10-inch platform that is just more than 3 feet longer than the SD40. Likewise, the SD40-2 truck centers are farther apart, measuring 43 feet, 6 inches, instead of 40 feet.

The SD40-2 epitomizes the product quality for which Electro-Motive is known. It rapidly became the standard locomotive of the 1970s and 1980s. Almost 4,000 were built for service in North America, making it by far the most common locomotive on American rails. The SD40-2 replaced less-reliable and poorer-performing locomotives and allowed some railroads to retire most of their first-generation road diesels. The success of the SD40-2 spelled the end of the line for many Alco Centuries and U-boats, some of which had just a decade of service behind them. By the early 1980s, the SD40-2 had become the ubiquitous symbol of heavy-freight railroading.

Praise for the SD40-2 has been loud and emphatic among railroaders. If you ask experienced locomotive engineers about their favorite machines, the SD40-2 is always mentioned. Engineer Craig Willett sums up the locomotive by saying, "It's a good-riding, good-pulling, and all-around good locomotive."

Below left: Canadian Pacific continued to order new EMDs with the 16-645E3 engine years after the introduction of the new 710G engine. The last 16-645 locomotives were CP's SD40-2Fs built in 1989. These locomotives featured a tapered variation of the cowl carbody. A westbound CP freight at Rock Glen, New York, catches the evening glint, highlighting a CP SD40-2 and SD40-2F. *Brian Solomon*

Below right: Canadian Pacific's SD40-2F No. 9024, seen here exiting Delaware & Hudson's Belden Tunnel on February 23, 2002, was the last locomotive of the SD40-2 line. At the time this locomotive was built, EMD's SD60 had been in production for nearly five years. *Tim Doherty*

7 Electro-Motive SD45T-2

Thunder in the canyon. An eastbound Southern Pacific freight negotiates the "Paired Track" in Nevada's Palisade Canyon on the morning of June 15, 1993. Leading the train, in order, are an SP SD40T-2, a Rio Grande SD50, two SP SD45T-2s, and a CSX SD40-2. Brian Solomon

A Rio Grande SD40T-2 leads a westbound intermodal train at Cedar, Utah, against a background of the Bookcliffs. Only Southern Pacific and Rio Grande bought SD40T-2s new from EMD. *Brian Solomon*

The Southern Pacific was characterized by sinuous steep mountain grades. In fact, as a result of its mountainous profile, SP had more tunnels than all of the other Western railroads put together. SP's named grades are famous in the annals of American railroading: Tehachapi, Cuesta, Siskiyou Summit, Cascade Summit, and, of course, Donner Pass.

Donner Pass, SP's Sierra crossing and a part of the original Transcontinental Railroad, was built in the 1860s and improved under the reign of E. H. Harriman after 1900. The brutal combination of long, sustained grades, high-altitude operation, tortuous track layout, and numerous tunnels and long snow sheds—necessitated by some of the heaviest annual snowfalls in North America—has made Donner Pass one of the most difficult places to run trains in the West. In the late steam era, SP was compelled to innovate the "cab-ahead" (or "cab-forward") design in order to permit the operation of powerful

"Mallet" articulated locomotives in the Sierra snow sheds. (In later years, SP operated a vast fleet of simple articulated steam locomotives using the cab-ahead design.)

In the early diesel era, SP looked to EMD F-units for its Sierra freight operations. The F effectively allowed SP to double the tonnage of freights crossing Donner Pass. In the early 1960s, Southern Pacific was enamored with high-horsepower, high-tractive-effort locomotives. It acquired the largest fleet of EMD SD45s and a substantial number of SD40s, as well as other high-horsepower models. While the big EMDs generally performed well for SP, their one flaw was when climbing through the Sierra tunnels. By this time many of the snow sheds that had mandated the cab-ahead design were gone, but enough sheds and tunnels remained to cause difficulties. Lifting a train over Donner means keeping a set of locomotives in Run 8 for mile after mile. The air-intakes on the EMD design are on top of the locomotive, which normally is not

a problem. But when working upgrade through high-altitude tunnels, the design results in very hot air being drawn into the engine, which can cause overheating that forces the locomotive to reduce power in order to protect itself. Consequently, performance suffers.

SP looked to find a cost-effective solution to this difficulty. According to John Garmany in *Southern Pacific Dieselization*, in the early 1970s, SP and EMD worked together to revise the airflow pattern on EMD's 20-cylinder, six-motor diesels. To suit the specialized requirements of the Southern Pacific, EMD built a unique fleet of 20-cylinder locomotives with their air-intakes relocated at midpoint above the rear truck. Garmany indicates that the modification improved power output in the Sierra tunnels by as much as 20 percent. The new model was designated SD45T-2 and, like the SD45, it was rated at 3,600 horsepower and incorporated other improvements of the DASH 2 line, including the improved electrical system and HTC trucks (see SD40-2).

The "T" in the new designation indicated the "tunnel" airflow arrangement, and the locomotives are known as "Tunnel Motors." According to *The Contemporary Diesel Spotter's Guide, 2000 Edition*, EMD built 247 SD45T-2s between 1972 and 1975. Later, Electro-Motive adapted the Tunnel Motor design to its 3,000-horsepower

Above: Fires raging in Idaho have spread a thin layer of dust in the atmosphere, which makes for an especially rosy Utah sunrise in September 1996. A westbound catches the glint at Solitude—a remote siding near Green River, Utah. *Brian Solomon*

Left: A quick external spotting difference between the otherwise very similar SD40T-2 and SD45T-2 are the number of panels above the low-level air intakes that characterize the "Tunnel Motor" type. An SD40T-2 (left) has two panels, while an SD45T-2 (right) has three. Traditionally, the more significant difference was under the hood and out of sight. An SD40T-2 used a 16-cylinder 645E3 engine, while an SD45T-2 had a 20-cylinder 645E3. However, following rebuilding, this was no longer a consistent difference. *Brian Solomon*

locomotive and built 310 SD40T-2s between 1974 and 1980. Both SP and the Denver & Rio Grande Western bought the locomotives.

Thomas M. Hoover was working for General Electric in the early 1980s when he participated on an exchange with SP that gave him the opportunity to study locomotive application and ride freights over Donner Pass. It was a rare privilege afforded to very few people beyond the ranks of SP.

On a glorious clear day, Hoover climbed aboard SP's RVNP-P at the yard in Roseville, California, for the run over Donner. The priority freight was run jointly with Union Pacific and carried California produce from Roseville to North Platte, Nebraska, in Pacific Fruit Express refrigerated boxcars. It was a remnant of what had once been a booming business. At one time SP moved a half-dozen or more solid fruit blocks eastbound out of Roseville every day. But by the early 1980s, the business had declined to little more than one train a day.

"We had four locomotives," Hoover recalls. "Leading was SP 9020, an SD45 that had just had a capital rebuild at the Sacramento Shops. SP went to the bank and this was basically a new locomotive. Behind it were two Tunnel Motors and another EMD. I rode the second unit. Our train weighed about 4,500 tons, so we didn't have a helper. Coming out of Roseville, the dispatcher came on the radio to tell us of a broken rail a little way to the east. We didn't encounter any difficulty and continued up the mountain. As we got higher up the mountain, I remember it being very smoky in the tunnels, but the highlight of the whole trip was at the top, where we were put into the siding at Norden to wait for a westbound."

Although the line over Donner had two main tracks, SP had Centralized Traffic Control at the top of the pass and often sent westbounds through Tunnel 41, "the big hole." In this manner, SP avoided routing them around the mountain on an old mainline that

Variations on a six-motor theme. An SP SD40T-2 Tunnel Motor leads an SD40 and an SD45 westbound at Floriston, California, on April 27, 1990. *Brian Solomon*

Three SP Tunnel Motors employed as the Lawton Helper are seen on a pleasant July evening at Shed 47 on the East Slope of Donner. *Brian Solomon*

Above: Doing the job for which they were built, three SD40T-2 Tunnel Motors and a lone SD40 lead a westbound train toward the summit of Donner Pass in the California Sierra. The train is about to enter the tunnels at Andover in Coldstream Canyon on the east slope of Donner. The Tunnel Motor was designed to combat the effects of high altitude operations in long tunnels in snow sheds by lowering the engine air-intake vents.
Brian Solomon

Opposite: It's a long way from California, baby, and you have a new dress and a new job. The Bessemer & Lake Erie acquired a fleet of remanufactured Southern Pacific SD45T-2s from the Boise Locomotive Company. These locomotives feature 16-cylinder 645 engines rated at 3,000 horsepower, instead of the 20-cylinder 645 that they were built with. B&LE 901, 907, and 903 lead a train at Butler, Pennsylvania, on December 26, 2000.
Patrick Yough

had traditionally been used as the westbound track, but which was a more difficult route than the big hole. Hoover continues:

> *We stopped just short of the sheds at Norden. When the westbound passed and we got the signal to go, our engineer cracked the throttle and we started east. What sticks in my mind, was I could feel the wheels biting into the sand. It really vibrated! In the days before automatic sanders, the engineer sanded by the ass of his pants. We started out slow and didn't make it to Run 8 until we were inside the sheds. You can imagine the noise! The tower man came on the radio as we passed the sheds, and shouted to the engineer, "You ol' Buffalo, you!" I guess that must have been his nickname. That "ol' Buffalo" made good time—we made it into Sparks early.*
>
> *On a return trip I was riding with some new General Electric B36-7s. By the nature of the GE design, all GEs are "Tunnel Motors." Going west, we stopped up on the mountain in the midst of a snowstorm to allow the rotaries [plows] to pass. When we got the signal to go, I was watching the ampmeter to see what would happen. I had heard lots of complaints about GEs being slow to load. Well, those SP 7700s went right to 1,000 amps—they powered right up.*

Several railroads have acquired rebuilt SP Tunnel Motors in recent years, among them Transtar railroads, Duluth, Missabe & Iron Range, and Bessemer & Lake Erie. Although they still use the SD45T-2 body, these locomotives have been substantially rebuilt: the 20-cylinder prime movers were replaced with 16-cylinder 645s. Electrical systems have been upgraded, and Q-Tron wheel-slip control installed to improve locomotive performance. Gordon Lloyd, Jr., Bessemer's manager of locomotive maintenance, indicates that three Tunnel Motors, now designated as SD40T-3s, can start a 10,358-ton ore train.

8 General Electric C30-7

Three Burlington Northern C30-7s and two SD40-2s lead a loaded Powder River coal train eastbound on BN's Black Hills subdivision at Mariette, South Dakota, on May 26, 1995.
Brian Solomon

Conrail had just 10 C30-7s, numbered 6600 to 6609, that were built in 1977. These six-motor GEs were often assigned to SENH/ NHSE (from Selkirk Yard near Albany, New York, to Cedar Hill yard near New Haven, Connecticut) freights. *Brian Solomon*

During the 1970s, the dynamics of the fuel market changed radically. The fuel crisis of 1973 and 1974 and again in the late 1970s drove the price of crude oil higher, and consequently the cost of diesel fuel rose. This sudden and dramatic price increase had a demonstrable effect on locomotive design. While locomotive fuel consumption was only a nominal concern prior to the fuel crisis, now it was a serious design concern. In the steam-to-diesel transition period, diesels were so much more efficient than steam that actual diesel fuel usage seemed immaterial. This sudden market change inherently favored General Electric diesels over General Motors—GE locomotives use a four-cycle engine that is inherently a more fuel-efficient machine than GM's two-cycle engine.

Yet GE's four-cycle engine had some drawbacks, too. Among the frequent complaints about GE diesels, however, is that they are much slower loading than GM's two-cycle engine. If you ask almost any railroader, they will quickly tell you that a GE has slower throttle response than a GM. Where an EMD seems to load almost instantly, GE's 7-FDL engine will take six to eight seconds to come up to speed—a delay known as "throttle-lag." While a delayed response may be annoying, for the railroad companies paying the bills slower throttle response is justifiable if it translates to much lower fuel consumption. In the bigger picture, a few seconds on the beginning of a long run won't make much difference to the bottom line of the company. As former General Electric design engineer Thomas M. Hoover put it, "If you are on the mountain with a lot of tonnage behind you, you can't use Run 8 anyway. So what's the difference how quickly the engine loads?"

Nominally lower performance is tolerable, so long as reliability is maintained. By contrast, if a locomotive isn't available for service—or worse, if it fails en route—better fuel economy suddenly doesn't matter anymore. While commonly seen as a "horsepower race," locomotive competition between EMD, GE, and Alco was more about reliability than horsepower. EMD's SD40, GE's U30C, and Alco's C630 produced the same output, but EMD's SD40 had much greater reliability. Guess which machine had the most sales? Guess which of these three companies exited the American market in the late 1960s as a result of its inability to compete?

GE's 1960s- and early-1970s-era Universal line, popularly known as "U-boats," had a reputation for poorer reliability than EMD locomotives. By the mid-1970s, many of GE's pioneering U25Bs, were little more than a decade old, but already ripe for retirement. By comparison, EMD locomotives over a decade older were being rebuilt for further service. General Electric gradually implemented design improvements that enhanced both reliability and performance.

In 1976, GE introduced new model designations to reflect the multitude of recent improvements to its locomotive line and distinguish its new machines from its older product line. With this change, GE dispensed with the Universal line and corresponding U Series designations

and debuted its DASH 7 line. In the new series, a 3,000-horsepower six-axle locomotive was designated the C30-7 instead of U30C. (The letter "C" indicates a six-axle six-motor truck, while "30" signifies 3,000 horsepower and "-7" represents 1977.) Among the DASH 7's selling points were improved fuel consumption, tighter hydrocarbon emissions, and greater overall locomotive reliability. Not all design improvements were introduced at once; instead they were implemented gradually. Some improvements had been implemented on late-era Universal locomotives and were carried over to the new DASH 7 line, while others debuted with the new line.

To improve fuel consumption, an eddy-current clutch (an electromagnetic clutch activated electrically) was installed to drive the radiator fan. The 18-millimeter double-helix fuel-injection pump became standard, replacing an older design. The advantage of this pump is that it varies injection timing with the quantity of fuel injected to improve fuel consumption at lower throttle positions. The 18-millimeter dimension refers to the diameter of the pump plunger.

Another fuel-saving feature was the use of a "skip three, double six" throttle schedule, which increased engine speed in the third, fourth, fifth, and sixth throttle positions (based on the traditional eight-position American Association of Railroads throttle) to reduce smoke emissions during acceleration. (Early GEs were notorious for their high smoke emissions when starting.) During the course of DASH 7 production, an engine sound muffler was also introduced to GE locomotive design to comply with federal sound emission regulations. These regulations are the primary reason why modern diesel locomotives make less noise than

Singing down welded rail at the maximum speed of 55 miles per hour near Bellville, Texas, a brakeman and conductor enjoy the breezy open-window ride in the cab of Burlington Northern C30-7 5568 on the fine spring evening of May 27, 1989. Although the C30-7 was designed for heavy-haul lugging in drag service, these units could get up and go when spurred, as evidenced by this scene. Three years later, this unit was upgraded from 3,000 to 3,300 horsepower by the railroad and given a class overhaul to extend the life of the locomotive an additional five years. *Tom Kline*

traditional models. Noise reduction has both good and bad effects, however. While quiet locomotives are less likely to offend sensitive ears and are less disturbing to people who live trackside, reduced sound emissions have made modern trains virtually silent, in some cases making them more dangerous to people trackside. Also, one man's noise pollution is another's music: the roars made by a U25B or a quartet of GP9s are sounds lost on modern ears.

The DASH 7 was a marked improvement over earlier GE diesels, and GE locomotive sales reflected this. In the DASH 7 era, GE made large gains in their domestic market share of new locomotive production, and in 1983 was able to outsell EMD for the first time. The most popular of the DASH 7 models was the six-motor C30-7, which was comparable to EMD's very popular SD40-2. According to figures in *The Contemporary Diesel Spotter's Guide*, GE built more than 1,100 C30-7s during the model's 10-year run, of which 783 were sold to American railroads. This was substantially more than any other General Electric model built up until that time.

The C30-7 employed the same principle components common to most large GE locomotives: a 16-cylinder 7FDL diesel engine and the latest version of GE's 752 Series traction motor. One variant of the C30-7 employed a 12-cylinder FDL engine and carried the C30-7A

designation, with the "A" indicating the smaller engine. Just 50 of these were built in 1984 for Conrail. According to GE specifications, the C30-7 measures 67 feet, 3 inches long; 15 feet, 4-1/2 inches tall; and 10 feet, 2-1/4 inches wide. It uses 40-inch-diameter wheels, and its weight varied depending on customer preference and the amount of fuel, water, and sand in the locomotive. (A heavier locomotive has greater tractive effort but requires a more substantial railroad line to accommodate it.) The maximum C30-7 weight is indicated as 420,000 pounds, all of which is carried on the 12 driving wheels. General Electric offered the model with three different gear ratios: 83/20 geared for 70 miles per hour, 81/22 for 79 miles per hour, and 79/24 for 84 miles per hour. The 70-mile-per-hour ratio was preferred.

Burlington Northern acquired the largest domestic fleet of C30-7s and used them largely for hauling coal trains originating at mines in Wyoming's Powder River Basin. Likewise, Norfolk & Western also had a sizeable fleet that it assigned to its coal traffic and other services. Union Pacific, CSX, and Conrail also operated C30-7s. According to *The Contemporary Diesel Spotter's Guide*, GE sold Nacionales de Mexico C30-7 "kits" for final assembly in Mexico. In addition, GE built C30-7s at its Erie, Pennsylvania, facility for both NdeM and Ferrocarril del Pacifico.

Left: On Southern Pacific, an amber-over-amber signal indicates "Approach Diverging," which means the train will proceed on a diverging route at the next signal. Here, a Union Pacific C30-7 leads an eastbound SP freight toward the west switch at Bealville in the California Tehachapis on March 20, 1994. This train will take the siding for a westbound freight that is holding the main track. *Brian Solomon*

Below: Burlington Northern C30-7 5074 rolls along near Pedro, Wyoming. *Brian Solomon*

9 Electro-Motive SD50

Under textured skies, Rio Grande SD50 5512 leads a unit coal train over Soldier Summit, Utah, on July 30, 1991. Electro-Motive's SD50s and GP50s were the first locomotives equipped with the "Super Series" wheel-slip system, which enhances performance at slower speeds. Brian Solomon

Above: In the fading glow of the winter sun, three former Rio Grande SD50s descend Soldier Summit, Utah. Brian Solomon
Left: During the Gulf War, Conrail specially decorated one of its SD50s to show support for American military forces.
Brian Solomon

The success of Electro-Motive's SD40-2 was a hard act to beat. That machine's consistently good performance and exceptional reliability has long made it popular with both railroads and railroaders. Despite the popularity of the SD40-2, EMD continued to push its design forward in an effort to obtain a locomotive with even better performance characteristics. In 1979, EMD built four SD40Xs for the Kansas City Southern using the latest 645 engine, designated the "16-645F," which generated 3,500 horsepower, 500 more horsepower than the 16-645E3 used in the SD40-2. Two years later, EMD introduced its new SD50 model, which also used the 16-645F and was initially rated at 3,500 horsepower. The SD50 remained in production from 1981 until 1985, and the rating of later locomotives was boosted to 3,600 horsepower.

Among the innovations introduced with the SD50 was the state-of-the-art "Super Series" wheel-slip control system that used a locomotive-mounted Doppler radar gun to measure track speed. The track speed

was compared with the speed of the wheels and the difference was used to compute the amount of wheel-slip control required. The radar used was similar to that employed by police for speed enforcement; as a result, the SD50's radar has been known to trip radar detectors in automobiles. The Super Series wheel-slip system enabled the SD50 to achieve 33 percent adhesion in ideal conditions, and EMD boasted that it permitted 24 percent adhesion even in poor conditions.

The SD50 didn't enjoy the same widespread popularity as the SD40-2, or even the SD45. A little more than 360 SD50s were built for domestic service, and 60 SD50Fs were built with a protective cowl body for the Canadian National. Although the SD50 suffered from a reputation of poor reliability, its relatively poor sales can also be attributed to the period in which it was produced. The recession of the early 1980s was hard on the railroads; traffic was down and thousands of locomotives were being stored nationwide. As a result, there was little need for new locomotives, and some lines continued to

Between 1983 and 1985, CSX ordered SD50s for its two component railroad networks, Chessie System and Seaboard System, which at that time still retained separate corporate images. The locomotives were numbered in the same sequence but painted in the different railroads' respective liveries. By the early 1990s, most of the SD50s had been repainted for CSX. Here, a pair of CSX SD50s leads an eastbound coal train on the Mountain Subdivision at Keyser, West Virginia, on October 23, order traditional SD40-2s even though the more powerful SD50 was available. In fact, it was during the production run of the SD50 (and four-motor GP50) that General Electric first surpassed EMD in locomotive production.

In the long run, the SD50 has not faired as well as the SD40-2. By 2001, as many SD50s had been sidelined and scrapped, while SD40-2s built in the 1970s were still working, some having been rebuilt more than once. The primary difficulty with the SD50 seems to have been its 16-645F engine. In a case of performance versus reliability and maintenance costs, extracting an additional 500 to 600 horsepower from the 645-engine design is reported to have taken a toll.

Conrail acquired one of the largest fleets of SD50s and frequently assigned them in pairs. Conrail engineer Don Jilson, however, ran SD50s over the Southern Tier Route (former Erie Railroad mainlines and connections across New York's Southern Tier region) and enjoyed working with them. "They had higher load ratings," Jilson explains. "Where an SD40 might be in the red at 1,000 to 1,200 amps, the SD50 could withstand 1,500 to 1,600 amps."

As a result of the higher horsepower, SD50s could make faster track speed than could SD40-2s in comparable circumstances. Jilson felt they ran better together, and when operating in pairs provided for a smoother-running consist. Overall, Jilson claims, SD50s were good locomotives from an engineer's viewpoint.

On a clear April afternoon, SD50s lead Conrail's BUOI (Buffalo, New York, to Oak Island, New Jersey) past venerable Union Switch & Signal semaphores at Arkport, New York. Although not as common as other EMD types, in the late 1980s SD50s were ubiquitous power on Conrail freights. Often run in pairs on the Water Level Route, SD50s were joined by additional locomotives for the run over the Southern Tier. *Brian Solomon*

10 General Electric C32-8

For nearly 15 years, the otherwise obscure General Electric C32-8 was a common site on Conrail's Boston Line. It's mid-morning on February 5, 1996, as a somewhat ratty-looking C32-8 leads a westbound over the Quaboag River west of Palmer, Massachusetts. Brian Solomon

Conrail C32-8 6617 leads a C36-7 and two C30-7As eastbound though the Twin Ledges near Middlefield, Massachusetts, in October 1991. *Brian Solomon*

The 10 General Electric C32-8s assigned to Conrail were a unique fleet of pre-production locomotives used as a test bed for later development; they were never duplicated in kind on Conrail, or anywhere else. The C32-8, however, represented a step toward producing a better locomotive.

While General Electric's early road diesels had a reputation of reliability problems, by the early 1980s, GE had more than two decades' experience in the road diesel market, was producing a substantially better product, and had gradually claimed a greater market share of domestic production from industry giant, General Motors. During the serious economic recession of the early 1980s when few new locomotives were ordered and thousands more were put in storage, General Electric's production matched that of General Motors'. And in 1983, for the first time, GE sold more new locomotives to American railroads than GM. It marked the first time since the end of the steam era that GM had held second place as a locomotive builder. Although GM was again selling the greater number of locomotives the following year, GE had initiated development of the DASH 8 locomotive line that

would make it America's dominant locomotive builder during the last decade of the twentieth century.

In 1982, General Electric built two prototypes that were the precursors to its DASH 8 line. One was a 3,600-horsepower four-axle model designated "B36-8," the other was a six-motor machine designated "C39-8." Like other modern General Electric high-horsepower diesels, both prototypes were powered by 16-cylinder FDL engines and used the latest generation 752 traction motor, the 752AG. What made the prototypes technologically significant was the pioneering use of microprocessors for locomotive control. Onboard computers and microprocessor control are considered by many locomotive historians as the defining elements of a third-generation diesel (the first generation being the machines that replaced steam, and the second being the high-powered machines introduced in the 1960s). While this is an overly simplistic method of classifying locomotives, it logically defines the stages of development.

In his article, "General Electric: A Prophecy Fulfilled," in the November 1988 issue of *TRAINS* magazine, Greg McDonnell

At dawn on August 11, 1985, Conrail BOEL (Boston, Massachusetts, to Elkhart, Indiana) approaches the east portal of State Line Tunnel on the old Boston & Albany Line near Canaan, New York. Leading is one of 10 C32-8s, locomotives that often operated on the B&A route. Today, this portal of State Line Tunnel is abandoned; all traffic uses the old eastward portal, which is on a slightly different alignment immediately to the south of this tunnel. *Brian Solomon*

explains that instead of building a traditional locomotive demonstrator to show off its new product line, General Electric built four small fleets of pre-production locomotives for road-testing by North American lines. Initially, General Electric retained ownership of the diesels, but had them painted and numbered for the railroads to which they were assigned: three B32-8s went to Burlington Northern, 10 C32-8s went to Conrail, three B39-8s were for the Santa Fe, and a pair of C39-8s went to Norfolk Southern (NS). While the B39-8 and C39-8 were powered by GE's 16-cylinder FDL, both the B32-8 and C32-8 used a 12-cylinder FDL engine. At the time, General Electric was promoting high-horsepower 12-cylinder locomotives for their fuel savings.

In addition to their groundbreaking microprocessor control, these new locomotives displayed an entirely new look that quickly distinguished them from General Electric's earlier machines. Since the 1960s, GE's domestic line used the classic rounded carbody and cab characterized by models such as the U30C. The introduction of the

DASH 7 line in the mid-1970s had not resulted in a substantive change in the look of the locomotives. There was no mistaking one of the new DASH 8s, however: they were clearly new and different. The rounded carbody had given way to a pronounced angular design with a boxed front end and slightly tapered nose. Large dynamic brake grids situated behind the cab, which still retained a curved roof profile on the pre-production units, gave the locomotives a beastly humpback appearance. This distinctive and raw yet attractive look earned the pre-production DASH 8s the nickname "Classics" at GE's shop in Erie, Pennsylvania. Production DASH 8s, introduced in 1987, did not feature classy elements like the rounded roofline, but displayed a starker, even more utilitarian look.

Conrail's C32-8s were delivered in autumn 1984 and carried the numbers 6610 to 6619. They came on the heels of a 50-unit order of C30-7As (numbered 6550 to 6599), which, like the C32-8s, used the 12-cylinder FDL and shared other common components.

Both the C32-8s and C30-7As were based at Conrail's Selkirk Yard south of Albany, New York, and were largely used on the heavily graded former Boston & Albany mainline that traversed the rolling Berkshire Hills. Since the earliest days of the Boston & Albany, the Berkshire grade challenged locomotive designers, and eventually went on to a long history as a test bed for new locomotive designs. In fact the "Berkshire"-type steam locomotive, the first of Lima's "superpower" designs, was named in honor of the West End grades, which it conquered in the 1920s.

Initially, the C32-8s worked in matched three-unit sets. Each locomotive produced 3,150 horsepower, giving a set 9,450 horsepower, enough to lift most trains over the Berkshires. Throughout the 1980s and early 1990s, the C32-8s and C30-7As were standard power on the Boston & Albany (B&A) route. Since the two types were very similar locomotives, they worked well together and were routinely assigned in mixed consists. By the late 1980s, sets of four of these GEs were common, and

by the early 1990s, other GE models were frequently mixed with them. The C32-8s often wandered from the B&A route and might be found just about anywhere on the Conrail system. At times they ran offline as part of a locomotive pool. They were also occasionally used offline for demonstration purposes. Greg McDonnell indicates that in 1986, two of the locomotives demonstrated on the Canadian National.

In the later days of Conrail, the C32-8s were assigned to *Ballast Express* service and dressed in a specialized all-gray livery that resembled the color of Conrail's ballast hoppers. A quarry along the B&A route in West Springfield, Massachusetts, provided much of the ballast for the system and, as a result, the C32-8s remained regular visitors on the line. When they were not hauling ballast, Conrail continued to assign them to conventional freights.

According the *Norfolk Southern Locomotive Directory 2001* by Paul K. Withers, NS has retired all 10 of their C32-8s and returned them to their lessor.

In April 1999, just a month before the dissolution of Conrail, a *Ballast Express* train rolls westbound through Mexico, Pennsylvania, on the old Pennsylvania Railroad Middle Division.
Michael L. Gardner

11 General Electric C36-7

Clouds roll in off Lake Ontario on a late Sunday morning in April 1989 as Conrail C36-7 6642 leads an SD50 and two U23Bs with an eastbound at School Road in Batavia, New York. Conrail had a small fleet of C36-7s that were part of its general road pool. Brian Solomon

The most powerful locomotive in General Electric's DASH 7 line was its C36-7, which was introduced as a 3,600-horsepower model, and later featured enhanced output rated at 3,750 horsepower. Instead of using an engine with a greater number of cylinders–the difference between EMD's 3,000-horsepower SD40 and 3,600-horsepower SD45–GE obtained more power in the C36-7 by changing the engine's fuel-rack settings. Overall, the C36-7 is mechanically the same as the C30-7: they use the same platform, engine, and other primary components.

The C36-7 was introduced in 1978, and like the C30-7, represented a significant improvement over its Universal line predecessor, the U36C. General Electric promoted the C36-7 for its fuel savings, improved mechanical and electrical components, and high-power performance. Among the C36-7 features were its 1616B4 turbocharger, better cooling grids for its dynamic brakes, steel-crown pistons, improved cylinder linings, a new lube oil pump, more-efficient fuel injection, an advanced variable-speed radiator fan, and the latest 752 Series traction motor design. Later C36-7s, those built after 1983,

incorporated sophisticated electronic control systems that had been tested on pre-production DASH 8 models and were actually built alongside the "classic" DASH 8s.

Although the C36-7 had more horsepower than the C30-7, an equally important consideration for railroads contemplating the model was its greater tractive effort. One of the most significant attributes of the later C36-7 was the SENTRY adhesion control system. Improved adhesion is a principle theme of many modern locomotive designs. Better adhesion provides higher tractive effort and, therefore, greater pulling ability at slow speeds. According to GE promotional literature, the SENTRY system used traction motor-shaft speed sensors in place of older axle-mounted systems. The motor shaft sensors were as much as six times more sensitive to speed fluctuations, allowing for more detailed corrections to wheel slip and better application of sand to the rail. Depending on the severity of wheel slip, the SENTRY system would automatically sand the rail, make small, calculated reductions to motor output to limit slipping, or in the most severe situations, reduce power output in order to maintain traction. The system was specially

Below: On March 23, 1989, Conrail C36-7 6623 leads an OIBU (Oak Island, New Jersey, to Buffalo, New York) westbound at Linden, New York. In the late 1980s, Conrail was routing several trains daily over its former Erie Railroad Southern Tier Line. In addition to Conrail traffic, Delaware & Hudson also operated several trains on the Erie Line between Buffalo and Binghamton, New York. *Brian Solomon*

Below right: A freshly painted Norfolk Southern C36-7 waits with a short double-stack train for a customs inspection at Black Rock in Buffalo, New York. *Brian Solomon*

designed to aid locomotive traction in poor weather conditions where wet rails result in greater wheel slip.

A related improvement was the GE-752AH traction motor, which GE stated had a higher continuous current rating than earlier 752 motors. Among the features of the new motor was better insulation, which allowed more copper to be wound on the armature coils, thus permitting a 6 percent rating increase over earlier designs. To minimize losses attributed to eddy currents, motor armature coils used a pair of conductors in parallel rather than a single conductor.

Between 1978 and 1985, General Electric built 129 C36-7s, the majority of which were the later, more powerful models with SENTRY

adhesion control. Although the C36-7 was not as popular as the C30-7, it was a transitional model during the early era of microprocessor control and an important evolutionary step in the development of the DASH 8, which became one of General Electric's most successful locomotive lines. The advanced systems used on the later C36-7s are comparable to similar technology employed by EMD on its 50 Series locomotives built during the same time frame. Norfolk & Western (and later Norfolk Southern), Union Pacific, and Conrail accounted for most of the domestic interest in the C36-7. Some were also built for railways in Mexico.

Eastbound on the old Western Pacific. Union Pacific C36-7 9004 and two C30-7s lead a manifest freight through the Chilcoot Tunnel at Beckworth Pass. Later production C36-7s, such as this one, were rated at 3,750 horsepower, 150 horsepower higher than earlier locomotives with the same model designation. *Brian Solomon*

12 Electro-Motive SD60

Against the backdrop of Arkansas' Black Fork Mountain, Kansas City Southern train No. 10 makes good time up the 1.35 percent Rich Mountain Grade under the command of engineer John Locke. Leading this hot New Orleans–Kansas City intermodal train is Electro-Motive Division SD60 716, one of the first production units of this 3,800-horsepower model, built in December 1989. Inside the cab, the crewmen in this October 11, 1993, scene wear David Clarke aircraft intercom headsets to protect their ears from the deafening roar of the 16-cylinder prime mover screaming at full throttle through the Ouachita Mountains. The SD60 was the first model to introduce the new 710G engine and use microprocessor controls in place of the usual modules and relays. Tom Kline

Above: CSX SD60 8705 is part of a three-unit helper shoving a coal train up the Cranberry Grade at Amblersburg, West Virginia, on October 27, 1991. CSX took delivery of 10 SD60s in 1989, and often assigned the locomotives to Grafton, West Virginia, for work on the Mountain Sub, the old Baltimore & Ohio West End. These SD60s were distinguished from the more common CSX SD50 by their lack of marker lamps on the nose of the cab. *Brian Solomon*

Above right: Another view of CSX SD60 8705 shows the unit in a more recent variation of the CSX livery. It is seen in October 1998 at Grafton, West Virginia, almost seven years after the photo of it at Amblersburg was made. *T. S. Hoover*

In 1984, Electro-Motive introduced its new line of 60 Series diesels. By far the most popular model of this line was the six-motor SD60. While the SD60's external appearance closely resembled the SD50 that debuted just four years earlier, it was significantly different in two key areas: First, it was the first locomotive to use EMD's new 710 Series diesel engine. Second, it was the first EMD production diesel to employ a wide range of microprocessor control systems to enhance locomotive performance and reliability.

The 710 diesel engine is an adaptation of the 1960s-era 645 engines and shares many common qualities with the 645 and its predecessor, the 567 engine. The external dimensions of the 710 engine were made only nominally larger than the 645, so it would not require a larger place inside the locomotive. EMD increased output by enlarging the cylinder stroke from 10 to 11 inches, giving each cylinder 710 cubic inches of displacement versus the 645 inches of

the earlier design. To make productive use of the greater displacement, EMD introduced its new Model G turbocharger and a better gas flow pattern. There were also many other small improvements with the 710 engine. According to an article by Dale Sanders titled "Super Series" in the October 1984 *CTC Board* magazine, the 710's cylinder liners were laser-hardened and the engine used a higher compression ratio (16:1) to improve exhaust gas scavenging at the end of the engine cycle and thus improve fuel efficiency. Fuel consumption, output, and reliability were all concerns with the new engine, as EMD was by this time facing more serious competition from General Electric. Where the 16-645F engine produced a maximum practical output of just 3,600 horsepower, the new 16-710G was rated at 3,800 horsepower. However, the new engine was more than just a nominally more powerful machine—its design was intended to correct reliability issues faced by the high-output 16-645F.

A more powerful engine required equivalent improvements to the electrical transmission system. As was the case when EMD introduced its new line of 645 diesels in the mid-1960s, the 60 Series locomotives featured an array of new electrical components, including the new AR15 alternator. Sanders notes that the AR15 is rated at 4,680 amperes, 480 amperes higher than the earlier AR10 alternator. In conjunction with the AR15, a better traction motor, the Model D87, was also introduced.

The use of microprocessor control systems reduced the number of locomotive electrical components by more than 20 percent. Microcircuits took the place of older solid-state electronics and relays for improved reliability. While computer controls allow for more effective engine and electrical component control, computerized diagnostic systems were designed to more effectively analyze locomotive performance flaws as they developed. As with the 50

Series, the 60 Series locomotives employed the Doppler-based Super Series wheel-slip control.

During 60 Series production, EMD made significant changes in its manufacturing process. In *TRAINS* magazine's forty-second annual "Motive Power Survey" published in October 1990, Greg McDonnell notes that, during 60 Series production, General Motors gradually shifted the bulk of its locomotive production from its traditional La Grange, Illinois, facility to its Diesel Division located in London, Ontario. Today, the bulk of its locomotive construction occurs at London, with La Grange playing just a support role; builder's plates on new locomotives reflect this change.

Another significant change that took place during production of the 60 Series was the introduction and adoption of the North American Safety Cab, a development discussed in greater depth in the section on SD60Ms.

Top right: Oakway provided Burlington Northern "power by the hour," using a fleet of 100 SD60s. These locomotives were painted in a blue-and-white scheme similar to EMD's demonstrator colors. On July 12, 1994, an Oakway SD60 and one of BN's own SD60Ms are seen with an empty coal train at Sentinel Butte, North Dakota, on the edge of the Badlands. *Brian Solomon*

Lower right: Soo Line SD60 6047 leads Guilford's EDMO (East Deerfield, Massachusetts, to Mohawk Yard, Schenectady, New York) across the Deerfield River Bridges at East Portal in Florida, Massachusetts. In a moment, this westbound freight will enter Boston & Maine's 4-3/4-mile-long Hoosac Tunnel. *Patrick Yough*

13 Electro-Motive GP60

Southern Pacific was among the last major railroads to embrace the high-horsepower, four-axle, four-motor locomotive for high-speed intermodal service. In 1994, it received its final order of GP60s, which were the last all-new four-axle freight locomotives built in the United States. A trio of SP GP60s leads an eastbound Sunset Route double-stack at Mons on the east slope of California's Beaumont Hill in January 1994. Brian Solomon

Electro-Motive's four-axle, four-motor road switcher was originally developed as a Universal locomotive, a purpose reflected in its GP (or "General Purpose") designation. The GP's utilitarian car body presented a sharp contrast to the streamlined E- and F-Units that had been the prevalent EMD road diesels until that time. The flexibility afforded by a bi-directional four-axle locomotive allowed railroads to assign GPs to just about any type of service: they could be used singly as switchers, on local freights and short passenger trains, or run in multiple in heavy freight service. This building-block method of assigning motive power meant that railroads could assign any number of locomotives to a train (as many as one dozen or more GPs have been used to move long freights).

The hood arrangement made for ease of maintenance and was significantly cheaper to purchase new than the full carbody Es and Fs,

two features that gave the GP a decided cost advantage over earlier types. By the mid-1950s, EMD's GP9 was the bestselling locomotive in America. By contrast, the six-axle, six-motor SD9 (Special Duty) road switcher was billed as a specialty locomotive. Gradually, the six-motor locomotive replaced the four-motor as standard motive power on American rails. Over the years, the GP evolved into a high-horsepower machine designed for fast intermodal service and other high-horsepower applications and by the mid-1980s, the new four-motor GP had become a specialized model.

In 1985, EMD introduced its GP60, a high-horsepower, four-axle model equipped with the new high-displacement 16-710G engine. It was rated at 3,800 horsepower, and designed for fast intermodal work. In modern times the market for such locomotives is fairly small, and Southern Pacific and Santa Fe (which prided itself in its premiere Chicago-to-California runs) ordered most of the production run. Southern Pacific often assigned its four-motor locomotives to its Sunset Route hotshots. GP60 production spanned nearly nine years, ending with an order from SP in 1994. As of this writing, these Southern Pacific GP60s were the last all-new four-motor locomotives built for heavy road service in North America.

Norfolk Southern acquired a small fleet of 3,000-horsepower GP59s, which utilized a fuel-efficient 12-cylinder 710G engine. These locomotives, which closely resembled the more powerful GP60, were also designed for high-horsepower work.

Santa Fe ordered two unique variations of the GP60. In 1990, the railroad took delivery of 63 GP60Ms, which featured the North American Safety Cab and were the only modern EMD four-motor locomotives with Safety Cabs designed for freight service. The locomotives were delivered in Santa Fe's colorful war bonnet livery and were supplemented one year later with 23 cabless GP60Bs, which were anomalies in modern American locomotive practice. In the F-Unit era, cabless boosters had been standard on most American railroads. With the advent of the road switcher, however, the need for boosters was greatly diminished, although both Union Pacific and Pennsylvania had ordered cabless GP9Bs. In more recent time, Santa Fe had built its own boosters from the remains of wrecked six-motor units.

The GP60 was primarily the tool of Western lines. With the megamergers of the mid-1990s, Burlington Northern inherited Santa Fe's GP60 fleet, while Union Pacific acquired Southern Pacific's, including three units assigned to the Rio Grande. One small user of GP60s today is the Vermont Rail System (VRS), which acquired a pair of Texas-Mexican GP60s in late 2000 or early 2001. These high-horsepower GPs are regularly assigned to the former Rutland Railroad route between Rutland and Bellows Falls, Vermont. Lifting a mixed freight over the winding Mt. Holly grade is a far cry from racing a long intermodal train across the Arizona desert, but VRS has been making good use of their GP60s.

Far left: Southern Pacific GP60s were standard power on the Sunset Route, where a high-horsepower-per-ton ratio was the order of the day on intermodal trains. Assigning more horsepower for each ton allows the train to maintain faster over-the-road time. *Brian Solomon*

Left: Santa Fe assigned its best locomotives to its highest priority trains. In May 1991, Santa Fe's westbound 199 train (Chicago to Richmond, California) behind four new GP60Ms hums through Collier, California, only a few miles from the yard at Richmond. The GP60M was effectively custom-built for Santa Fe, as the railroad was closely involved with the development of the Safety Cab used on the GP60M. No other railroad ever ordered any locomotives of this type. *Brian Solomon*

14 General Electric
DASH 8-40C

General Electric's successful DASH 8 locomotive line allowed GE to race forward as America's premier diesel locomotive builder. Beneath a clear Wyoming sky on September 26, 1989, Union Pacific DASH 8-40C heads eastward toward North Platte, Nebraska. Brian Solomon

Far left: The view from the old Western Maryland Viaduct at Meyersdale, Pennsylvania, shows CSX DASH 8s working eastbound with an auto-rack train toward Sand Patch on the old Baltimore & Ohio. Brian Solomon

Left: A CSX DASH 8-40C crests the grade at Sand Patch, Pennsylvania, in October 1992. Brian Solomon

Silhouetted by the evening sun, a Chicago &
North Western DASH 8-40C leads a loaded
coal train south of Bill, Wyoming. With the
DASH 8, General Electric was able to
convince dyed-in-the-wool EMD customers
such as C&NW to buy its diesels.
Brian Solomon

In 1987, General Electric initiated regular production of its DASH 8 line with the six-motor DASH 8-40C. Innovations that had been tested on pre-production DASH 8 models such as Conrail's C32-8s became standard features of the new line. The most significant innovation of the DASH 8 line was its widespread use of onboard computers. Through microprocessor control, General Electric honed locomotive performance and increased component reliability.

Railway technology has long been closely tied to early computer development. Centralized Traffic Control machines developed in the 1920s for the remote-control operation of signals with electrical interlocking relays were a precursor to the first computers developed during World War II for code breaking. Although computers had been used for other aspects of railway operations, they did not become an integral part of locomotive control until the 1980s. By that time, computer technology had become sufficiently reliable and durable to withstand railroads' difficult and rugged operating environments, and small enough to be conveniently placed within the confines of a locomotive.

Three computers are used on the DASH 8: one to oversee locomotive control functions, one to manage the main alternator, and one to control fan and blower motors. These computers employ programs to exact optimal performance from respective locomotive components while protecting systems from harmful overuse. Diagnostic features, meanwhile, track and record component performance while monitoring external conditions. In this way, flaws can be detected before they become serious enough to result in damaged equipment. By employing sensors to monitor and compare engine speed, traction motor current, axle speed, and the status of the engineer's controls, in addition to other information, onboard computers can calculate the condition of locomotive performance. If these conditions are deemed hostile to the equipment, the computer will automatically de-rate (scale back) engine output to prevent damage.

With the extremely high cost of new locomotives and the great cost of locomotive repair, computer controls are intended to enable railroads to make the most of new motive power while minimizing repair costs. Computer control has also simplified locomotive operation. With new control systems, a locomotive engineer is less likely to damage a locomotive through improper operation. Conversely, one trade-off of computer control is that an element of human control has been sacrificed.

Three General Electric locomotives on Chicago & North Western display the progression of model types. A conventional cab DASH 8-40C leads a DC traction DASH 9-44CW and an AC traction AC4400CW on a very heavy unit coal train south of Bill, Wyoming. On the back of this train is another DASH 8-40C shoving hard as a helper. *Brian Solomon*

Some locomotive engineers find that this detracts from their ability to properly run trains. Despite the best intentions of a computer's program, a computer does not always make the best decisions on every occasion. For example, an onboard computer may shut down a locomotive on the road for the wrong reasons. This happens at inopportune times; at best, it slows a train's progress, but in more difficult situations it can result in a stall. When a train stalls, goods are delayed and costs go up. Despite occasional computer failures and related problems, the use of microprocessors has been beneficial overall, and permitted the development of far more efficient locomotives.

To underscore the significance of its new locomotive line, General Electric changed its locomotive designation scheme. The new engines were literally called DASH 8s, followed by a two-digit number indicating horsepower output, and a "B" or "C" to indicate the number of powered axles. This designation system change was not universally accepted and many railroads continued to use the older style of designations, which has produced some confusion over the years. For example, on some lines a DASH 8-40C, may be known as a C40-8.

General Electric's DASH 8 line has been an enormous success for the company. Higher performance coupled with greater reliability contributed to General Electric becoming the largest supplier of new locomotives for the American market, a position it had held briefly in 1983. In addition to supplying traditional customers such as Union Pacific, Conrail, and CSX with large orders of DASH 8 locomotives, GE convinced railroads like Chicago & North Western, which had relied primarily on EMD locomotives for many years, to purchase new GE DASH 8s.

15 Electro-Motive SD60M

The North American Safety Cab made its public debut on a freight locomotive with Union Pacific's SD60M in 1989. Although "wide-nose" cabs had been used on the DDA40X and Canadian models, the Safety Cab is a modern innovation for freight power in the United States. On September 26, 1989, this new UP SD60M was a novelty; today, the Safety Cab is a standard feature on all new locomotives. Brian Solomon

There's nothing like the polarized clarity of a clear winter day in New England. On January 11, 1998, Conrail 5502 leads TV10B eastbound at Palmer, Massachusetts. Conrail's wide-nose cabs all used the two-piece windshield. *Brian Solomon*

One of the most significant changes in the appearance of modern locomotives has been the widespread adoption of the North American Safety Cab, also described as "comfort cabs" and "wide cabs." Prior to 1989, the vast majority of locomotives in the United States used what is now termed a "conventional cab." In the late 1950s and early 1960s, railroads went from using locomotives with high short hoods (although this seems incongruous, "high" refers to the height of the hood, while "short" refers to the length) to low short hoods. From about 1962 onward, most locomotives were built with low short hoods, with the exception of locomotives ordered by Southern Railway and Norfolk & Western, two lines that continued buying high short hoods for almost another two decades. Notable exceptions to the

conventional cab were the cowl-style cabs used on locomotives such as the FP45, DDA40X, and F40, and the "Canadian Cab" first ordered by the Canadian National in the early 1970s. Both of these designs used a full-width nose and are obviously the antecedents to the present-day North American Safety Cab.

What changed and what were the first railroads to use the modern Safety Cab? During the 1970s and 1980s, numerous changes in railway labor practices changed the way railroads ran trains. Starting about 1983, major railroads began eliminating cabooses at the end of trains, resulting in less space where crewmembers could ride. Railroads made agreements with labor unions to reduce train crew sizes in conjunction with the elimination of caboose operation. At one time, a five- or six-man

crew was required for freight train operation, but with modern technology and contemporary operation patterns, most through freights could operate safely with just two- or three-man crews.

In addition to trimming crew size, railroads also pressed to lengthen crew districts. Traditionally, crew districts were roughly 100 miles long. In steam days this practice was logical, but by the 1980s the arrangement was obsolete and required railroads to employ far more operating personnel than was really needed to move trains over the road. Santa Fe, known for running fast freight, was among the first of the large railroads to negotiate with its unions to reduce crew sizes and increase the length of crew districts. As a concession to operating personnel, Santa Fe agreed to provide crews with better

work environments, including better locomotive cabs. In his article "Cab of the Future" in the December 1990 issue of *TRAINS* magazine, Steve Schmollinger listed objectives that Santa Fe and its crews desired from a new cab design, including a safer, quieter space with more ergonomic arrangements for the locomotive engineer.

Although modern road locomotives evolved from the road switcher type, in modern operation very little switching is actually performed with road locomotives. The cab and control arrangements that made sense for a road switcher were no longer adequate for engineers who faced forward for hours at a time. Schmollinger notes that Santa Fe borrowed a modern Canadian National SD50F for evaluation, while drawing inspiration from its own FP45/F45s in coming up with the design

At sunset on June 12, 1993, Union Pacific 6237 leads an eastbound stack train down Encina Hill in eastern Oregon.
Brian Solomon

for a new, modern cab. Santa Fe also considered a modern cowl-type locomotive along the lines of those used by Canadian roads, but decided against it. Instead, they worked with both General Motors and General Electric to design what evolved into the North American Safety Cab.

The new cab incorporated soundproofing, desktop controls, a better forward view, and greater structural safety to protect crews in the event of a collision. Initially, Santa Fe was interested in Safety Cab, high-horsepower four-axle units for its fast Chicago-California intermodal trains. By 1990, both GM and GE had built such locomotives to fit Santa Fe's needs—GM providing its GP60M (the "M" indicating "Modified") and GE its DASH8-40BW (with "W" indicating the Safety Cab). However, as it happened, the first American freight locomotive to take advantage of new Safety Cab improvements was actually the six-

axle SD60M, a type first ordered by Union Pacific, a road which, like the Santa Fe, had a historical interest in wide-nose designs.

Union Pacific's SD60M entered service during the early part of 1989. The locomotive featured an early version of EMD's North American Safety Cab which had a three-piece windshield and is clearly related to the cab style used on both Canadian Pacific's SD40F-2 that entered production in late 1988 and EMD's F59 commuter rail locomotive. Soo Line and Burlington Northern also bought SD60Ms with the three-piece windshield. EMD later refined its Safety Cab design, introducing a more uniform-looking two-piece windshield and tapered nose, among other improvements.

Santa Fe's interest in high-horsepower four-axle locomotives with Safety Cabs was unique to that line. It was the only American railroad to buy such machines for freight service, although Amtrak bought virtual duplicates of Santa Fe's wide-nose GEs for its passenger operations. In contrast to Santa Fe's specialized machines, six-motor DC traction locomotives with Safety Cabs were standard models in the early 1990s. Although railroads such as the Illinois Central and Norfolk Southern continued to purchase the older style of cab, most American lines opted for the Safety Cab when it became available. A variation of the SD60M is the SD60I, which uses EMD's WhisperCab (also known as the "isolated cab," signified by the letter "I" in the model designation) to provide greater soundproofing. Locomotives so equipped are identifiable by the visible separation in the metal between the cab and locomotive nose.

From a mechanical perspective, the SD60M is no different from the SD60. The locomotives use the same type of engine and electrical systems. The assignment of the locomotives varied from line to line, though. Union Pacific and Conrail bought SD60Ms for general service and routinely assigned them to their road pools for general mainline service. By contrast, Burlington Northern bought a fleet of SD60Ms specifically for mineral service. They were initially based at Glendive, Montana, and primarily employed in Powder River coal service, although a few locomotives also worked iron ore trains operating from Minnesota's Iron Range to Birmingham, Alabama.

When the SD60Ms were new in 1989, they were a novelty on American rails. The unusual cab style quickly set them apart from other locomotive types. This perception changed with the immediate popularity of the Safety Cab design. By the mid-1990s, locomotives with Safety Cabs were becoming predominant, and by 2002 locomotives without Safety Cabs were unusual. In just a decade, the face of American railroading was changed.

Electro-Motive's early SD60Ms had a three-piece windshield that resembled the windshield arrangement on some of its export models. Here, a UP SD60M passes Eccles siding in Nevada's Clover Creek Canyon on the Los Angeles & Salt Lake Route. *Brian Solomon*

16 General Electric DASH 8-40CW

It's a sunny day in the Windy City as Conrail DASH 8-40CWs pose in the shadow of Chicago's Sears Tower on March 4, 1995. Conrail, always a large General Electric customer, received its first DASH 8-40CWs in 1990. By the mid-1990s, they were among the most common types of road power on the system. Unfortunately, the locomotives did not weather well and spent much of their careers wandering in faded paint. Brian Solomon

Although EMD was the first locomotive manufacturer to adopt the North American Safety Cab for domestic commercial production, General Electric also adopted a variation of the cab style. In 1988, a four-motor prototype was built at Erie, Pennsylvania, and in 1990 GE began building DASH 8-40CWs for Union Pacific (the "W" in the designation indicating the new wide-nose cab). General Electric's Safety Cab features a simpler front window arrangement than EMD's later cabs. Initially, EMD used a three-window design that was adapted from cabs used on Canadian locomotives, and later used a two-window arrangement featuring a pair of trapezoidal windows and a tapered front nose with slightly rounded corners. By contrast, GE employed two rectangular windows with a more angular front end than that used by EMD.

Within a year of the DASH 8-40CW's introduction, Conrail, Santa Fe, and CSX had ordered units from General Electric. While the Safety Cab was initially offered as a customer option, shortly after its debut most new General Electric locomotives were being built with Safety Cabs. Introduced on the DASH 8, the wide-nose feature has since been carried over to GE's DASH 9 and AC model lines. In fact, today, General Electric Safety Cab locomotives have become the most prevalent designs in North America.

The basic DASH 8-40CW is essentially the same mechanically as the DASH 8-40C. According to *The Contemporary Diesel Spotter's Guide*, both locomotives measure 70 feet, 8 inches long, with 43-foot, 4-inch truck centers. Primary components are the same, including a 16-cylinder FDL engine that produces 4,000 horsepower for traction. Although many GE Safety Cabs have a very similar appearance, subtle internal and external variations between different orders are specific to different customers' needs.

Santa Fe's first Safety Cab GEs were four-axle DASH 8-40BWs that were designed for high-speed intermodal service and delivered in late 1990 and early 1991. As in the case of EMD's GP60Ms designed for the same purpose, the DASH 8-40BWs were delivered in Santa Fe's flashy war bonnet livery and numbered in the 500 Series. In 1992, Santa Fe took delivery of its first six-axle DASH 8-40CWs, numbered in the 800 Series. According to *Diesel Era*, these locomotives were delivered with a 3,800-horsepower rating at Santa Fe's request and rode on 42-inch wheels instead of 40-inch.

Left: On June 12, 1993, Union Pacific 9475 leads an eastbound K-Line toward the Leonard Horseshoe located between Durkee and Oxman, Oregon, on Encina Hill. This locomotive is a GE DASH 8-40CW, which is rated at 4,100 horsepower and ballasted to 399,000 pounds, according to the *Union Pacific Locomotive Directory 2000*. UP classifies this type of locomotive as a C41-W—today, some railroads use locomotive designations that are different from those used by the manufacturers. *Brian Solomon*

Right: Tim Doherty captured CSX GEs on the National Docks secondary in Jersey City, New Jersey, in November 1999. In less than two years' time the New York City skyline would be forever changed. *Tim Doherty*

There were also other noteworthy differences between Santa Fe's DASH 8-40CW and other locomotives of the type. Santa Fe intended to use some of the locomotives for coal service in northern New Mexico's York Canyon. In order to accommodate dimensional constraints imposed by the coal-loading equipment at York Canyon, all of the 800-class locomotives featured a slightly different cab roofline. The locomotives specifically assigned to coal service were also equipped with slow-speed motor controls for the loading of trains. Some later six-motor DASH 8s ordered by Santa Fe and Union Pacific featured an improved radiator design known as "split cooling" (see DASH 9). These locomotives had a slightly higher horsepower rating of 4,135 and, accordingly, are sometimes designated DASH 8-41CWs.

The success of the DASH 8 design encouraged Canadian National's first order for GE road diesels. The locomotives were designated DASH 8-40CMs and built to CN specifications, featuring a full-width cowl carbody and a Canadian variation of the Safety Cab with four front windshields. It also rode on Dofasco trucks instead of GE's "Adirondack" design. As a result, DASH 8-40CMs are slightly longer and have slightly different truck centers. These modifications give the locomotives a significantly different appearance than other General Electric locomotives.

At one time Baltimore & Ohio and Western Maryland competed for traffic moving west of Baltimore over the Alleghenies. The two railroads were parallel in many places. West of Cumberland, the B&O followed a northerly route by way of Sand Patch, while WM followed a southerly alignment. At Keystone—pictured here with a westbound CSX freight—the two alignments crossed over one another. Today, the Western Maryland is largely abandoned and its route fragmented, while the B&O line is a CSX mainline. *Brian Solomon*

17 Electro-Motive SD70

Conrail's 2500 Series SD70s were delivered to Norfolk Southern specifications, which included a conventional cab and control stand. A pair of new SD70s works a westbound between Spruce Creek and Union Furnace, Pennsylvania, in November 1998. Six months later, this route became part of the NS system. Brian Solomon

The SD70M has become Union Pacific's standard general-service locomotive, gradually taking the place of the SD40-2. A quartet of UP SD70Ms leads an eastbound intermodal train along Caliente Creek near the town of Caliente in the California Tehachapis. *Michael L. Gardner*

Electro-Motive's SD70M debuted in late 1992 with a three-unit demonstrator set wearing a new livery. The striking metallic maroon-and-silver paint had a decidedly automotive appearance to it, appropriate perhaps to a General Motors product line, but an odd color selection for the railroad world.

The SD70M and the other 70 Series variations represent the pinnacle of General Motors' DC traction development for heavy freight service. The SD70M appeared on the scene just a year before the far more significant SD70MAC, General Motors' pioneering AC traction

model that set the trend for locomotive sales and development in the mid-1990s. In its first years, the SD70M took a back seat to new AC models. However, in the year 2000 an enormous order from Union Pacific for 1,000 DC traction SD70Ms made the model one of General Motors' bestselling contemporary diesel locomotives.

Where the mechanical differences between the SD50 and SD60—the introduction of a new prime mover, new electrical components, and microprocessor control—represented a distinct jump forward in General Motors' locomotive technology, the SD70M featured

Canadian National's SD70Is came equipped with EMD's WhisperCab, which provides added soundproofing between the cab and the rest of the locomotive. On October 15, 1995, a pair of brand-new CN SD70Is rolls along the Mississippi River on the Burlington Northern Santa Fe. *Brian Solomon*

On a clear October afternoon, a Norfolk Southern SD70 and two GEs lead a loaded Bow coal train east at North Pownal, Vermont. *Brian Solomon*

With the SD70M, Union Pacific reintroduced its classic blue "wings" on the front of its locomotives. A variation of this livery was standard on its early diesels. *Brian Solomon*

Above: Norfolk Southern locomotives often run through on coal trains to Guilford's Boston & Maine route. In October 2001, NS SD70 2561 leads an empty Mt. Tom coal train at South Deerfield, Massachusetts. *Brian Solomon*

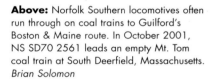

Opposite: A vision of things to come. Resting quietly in the sodium-vapor glow of Southern Pacific's West Oakland Diesel Shop, EMD's SD70M demonstrators make their rounds on the SP in June 1993. At the time, SP had only ordered locomotives with conventional cabs, but soon ordered fleets of new six-motor safety cabs from both EMD and General Electric. *Brian Solomon*

just nominal improvements over the SD60M. According to a feature story by Paul D. Schneider in the January 1993 issue of *TRAINS*, some of the SD70M's basic improvements included a horsepower boost from 3,800 to 4,000 using a 16-cylinder 710G3B engine; an upgraded model D90TR traction motor capable of maintaining 109,000 pounds of continuous tractive effort; and a more advanced microprocessor control system. Although the difference in output is almost insignificant in actual locomotive application, the SD70M's nominal horsepower increase allowed Electro-Motive Division's standard road diesel to match the output of General Electric's DASH 8-40C/DASH8-40CW.

The most significant—and the most visible—improvement introduced on the SD70M was Electro-Motive Division's new HTCR (High-Tractive C-type truck [three-axle] Radial) "self-steering" or "radial" truck. The new three-axle design allowed movement of the center axle to permit the truck to negotiate curves far more efficiently than earlier designs. By steering into curves, the radial truck greatly reduces friction between wheel and rail, resulting in lower wheel and rail wear and greater adhesion. Lower wear reduces maintenance cost for both the locomotive and track structure, while greater adhesion permits higher tractive effort. The SD70M was the first production

locomotive to use a self-steering truck, but most subsequent EMD six-axle diesels for the domestic market have been equipped with the HTCR truck. To emphasize the significance of the HTCR, some locomotives so equipped, like Conrail's SD80MAC, had the word "Radial" painted on the locomotive cab.

A few years after the debut of the SD70M, General Electric also introduced a self-steering truck design that can be found on a number of GE's newest AC traction locomotives, including AC4400CWs built for Canadian Pacific and Kansas City Southern, and CSX's AC6000CWs and some of its AC4400CWs.

In 1993, Electro-Motive's SD70Ms made a demonstration tour of major railroads. Southern Pacific, which was chronically power short and in desperate need of new locomotives, took special interest in the new model. At times, the railroad was leasing 300 or more locomotives a day to handle surging traffic levels and to make up for deficiencies in its aging and often poorly maintained fleet. Southern Pacific was the first customer for the SD70M, purchasing 25 of them in 1994, along with a large number of rebuilt EMD six-motor locomotives from MK Rail and an order for General Electric DASH 9s. Initially, Southern Pacific primarily assigned its new SD70Ms to its Los Angeles–to–Portland, Oregon, "I-5 Corridor" (so-named by SP's marketing people for the Interstate highway that ran roughly parallel to SP's tracks). Canadian National ordered a variation of the SD70M that used the WhisperCab and thus was designated SD70I.

By the mid-1990s, although most American railroads were ordering Safety Cabs, Illinois Central and Norfolk Southern did not find that the feature represented a cost advantage for their operations, and both lines ordered SD70s with conventional cabs. Prior to the dissolution of Conrail at the end of May 1999, the railroad received new locomotives built to the specifications of both Norfolk Southern and CSX, the two railroads that agreed to split Conrail. CSX desired AC traction SD70MACs, while Norfolk Southern preferred DC traction SD70s with conventional cabs. Conrail's 24 SD70s, numbered in the 2500 Series consistent with NS' numbering scheme, were assembled at the railroad's former Pennsylvania Railroad Juniata Shops at Altoona, Pennsylvania.

Union Pacific's SD70Ms are interesting because they represent a return to traditional technology and are, in effect, modern incarnations of the SD40-2. Analog engineer's controls are used in place of modern desktop electronics and mechanical fuel injection is used instead of electronic fuel injection. To make an automotive comparison, imagine General Motors reintroducing its 1970s Chevy Nova because it found customers were dissatisfied with the performance and reliability of modern gadgetry on contemporary cars.

The UP SD70M answers the complaints of many in the industry that have long held the SD40-2 in high regard. Yet some industry insiders indicate that GM's strategy may only be a short-term motive power solution. It is questionable if new locomotives such as UP's "retro" SD70M will comply with increasingly strict engine emission requirements imposed by state and federal authorities.

The large numbers of new UP SD70Ms have allowed the railroad to retire older locomotives, including UP's more obscure types, many of which were inherited from Chicago & North Western and Southern Pacific in mergers of 1995 and 1996. UP's SD70Ms are noted for their dependability, and with 1,000 of them on order, Union Pacific will have a relatively uniform fleet of road locomotives. From Chicago to Los Angeles, from New Orleans to Seattle, and from San Francisco to Denver, Union Pacific SD70Ms are now standard power. They haul heavy tonnage over Tehachapi, stacks across the Sunset Route, and manifest trains over Sherman Hill. About the only thing SD70Ms don't haul much of is Powder River coal, traffic that is largely the domain of Union Pacific's AC fleet.

Today, Union Pacific is one of the oldest surviving names in American railroading, and with the SD70M, Union Pacific paid homage to its heritage by reintroducing its colorful blue-and-white "wings" on the front of its locomotives. The SD70Ms were the first new locomotives painted with wings in roughly three decades, but now many older types are being repainted with the design as well.

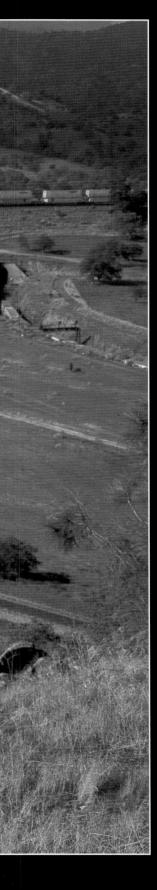

18 General Electric DASH 9

It's November 3, 2001, at the world-famous Tehachapi Loop near Keene, California, where four General Electric DASH 9-44CWs and a GP60M still in old Santa Fe paint lead a Burlington Northern Santa Fe eastbound freight up the mountain. The Tehachapi Loop is a complete spiral that allows the railroad to gain 77 feet in elevation over a relatively short distance. Michael L. Gardner

Enjoying a commanding view from the spacious comfort cab of a brand-new Santa Fe General Electric DASH 9-44CW 677, engineer Len Hitchcoth pilots a unit grain train east down the rails of the Galveston Subdivision through Rosenburg, Texas, on September 11, 1994. These centrally heated and cooled locomotive cabs feature the recently introduced desktop control stand and have such amenities as high-back adjustable seats, a refrigerator, a conductor's desk, and increased soundproofing for a quieter ride. Tom Kline

It's November 1993, and inside Building 10 at General Electric Transportation System's Erie, Pennsylvania, locomotive works, shop men dash about their duties against the cacophony of machine noise echoing throughout the enormous erecting haul—a virtual industrial symphony of whirring electrical motors, clanking metal, and the occasional shout. Basking in the flickering pinkish glow of bright sodium lamps rests the focal point of our visit to Erie: a brand-new Safety Cab locomotive, Chicago & North Western's first, but, more important, the *very* first of GE's newest marketing line: its DASH 9. Soon, this massive machine, 200 tons of steel, 73 feet, 6 inches long and 15 feet, 7.6 inches

tall, will head to the paint shop where it will be dressed in North Western's final livery—a yellow-and-green adaptation of its early diesel paint scheme. In a few months' time, C&NW DASH 9s will be based in the windy wilds of Bill, Wyoming, and assigned to Powder River coal service. What makes this machine different from the run-of-the-mill DASH 8? Why is the DASH 9 significant?

General Electric assigned the DASH 9 product name to its latest, and possibly its last, DC traction locomotive line. The DASH 9 debuted just a short time before the introduction of GE's AC4400CW, the manufacturer's first AC traction model and much bigger locomotive news.

The DASH 9 designation reflected a number of evolutionary improvements that GE had implemented as standard features on its DC locomotive line. GE's DASH 9 expanded on DASH 8 technology to provide a more capable locomotive with lower life cycle costs. Among the improvements were electronic fuel injection and split cooling, both of which had been tested on late-era DASH 8 models and were made standard with the DASH 9. General Electric also debuted a new and distinctive-looking high-adhesion truck to improve tractive effort. Other nominal improvements included a modified step and handrail arrangement for increased crew safety and comfort.

Electronic fuel injection (EFI) replaced conventional mechanical fuel injection systems in order to facilitate optimal engine combustion through calculated variation in fuel injection timing. The intention of EFI is more complete combustion resulting in improved fuel economy and reduced emissions. EFI also allows the elimination of some traditional components used by mechanical fuel injection, lowering maintenance costs and improving reliability. Government regulations on engine emissions are gradually becoming tighter, making lower emissions a significant design goal on new locomotives by both General Electric and General Motors. Radiators with the split

Southern Pacific DASH 9s lead an ore train over Wisconsin Central in February 1995. In just a few months these new DASH 9s would give way to even newer AC4400CWs on the high-priority taconite business handled by SP and WC between northeastern Minnesota's Iron Ranges and steelworks at Provo, Utah. With the arrival of AC4400CWs, SP reassigned DC traction DASH 9s to its Sunset Route. *Brian Solomon*

115

cooling arrangement are an important part of GE's strategy for lowering emissions. The term "split cooling" refers to the dual water circuits designed for the greater cooling of the diesel engine's intercoolers. Improved intercooler performance allows for lower air intake temperatures, which reduce emissions. An external feature that identifies GE locomotives with split cooling is slightly thicker radiator wings at the back of the locomotive. The wings house the radiator cores, which are 9 inches thick, 3 inches thicker than earlier designs. In conjunction with split cooling, GE also employed a coalescer in the crankcase ventilation system to filter oil vapors from exhaust gases.

Chicago & North Western's DASH 9s, and most subsequent models, were built as DASH 9-44CWs using 7FDL-16 engines with a 4,380-horsepower rating. (An exception is the large number of Norfolk Southern DASH 9s outlined in the General Electric DASH 9-40CW section.) Based on information in Sean Graham-White's "AC Revolution" in the January 1996 issue of *Pacific RailNews*, a DASH 9-44CW with standard options and 40-inch wheels with a 83:20 gear ratio can produce 140,000 pounds of maximum tractive effort and 108,600 pounds continuous tractive effort (calculated using a 27 percent factor of adhesion).

In the first half of 1994, Southern Pacific, Santa Fe, and Union Pacific also bought new DASH 9s, while CSX acquired a fleet of hybrid locomotives. Numbered in the 9000 Series and rated at 4,380 horsepower (4,400 horsepower in some sources), these unusual models

Canadian National ordered a variation of the DASH 9 that featured a slightly different cab configuration to meet Canadian specifications. Among the noticeable differences with the DASH 9-44CWL is a four-piece windshield instead of the standard two-piece windshield. On April 2, 1995, a brand-new CN DASH 9 leads an eastbound freight along the Mississippi River at Savanna, Illinois. *Brian Solomon*

Far left: Notice the small BNSF lettering below the road number in this low-angle view of the cab of Burlington Northern Santa Fe DASH 9-44CW 4726. It indicates that the unit was delivered in January 1998 from the General Electric factory in basic green-and-orange paint without the yellow lettering and striping decals. This was done to place the unit into immediate service during a motive power shortage on the railroad. After the shortage ended, the unit's decals were applied, completing what is referred to as the Heritage II scheme, seen here at Bellville, Texas, on July 2, 1998. *Tom Kline*

Left: Canadian National's later DASH 9-44CWLs featured larger lettering on the cab nose than the first order. CN 2565 leads a westbound across the bridge at Henry House, British Columbia, in the summer of 1998. *Eric T. Hendrickson*

straddled the DASH 8/DASH 9 production period and feature characteristics of both model lines. Since they do not ride on new high-adhesion trucks, they are not considered true DASH 9s. Southern Pacific assigned its DASH 9 fleet to some of its highest profile trains. In autumn 1994, SP and Wisconsin Central made industry news when they secured a lucrative iron ore contract between Minnesota's Iron Range and steelworks in Utah. This business had previously moved on a Union Pacific–Chicago & North Western routing. By keeping its ore trains on a tight schedule and cleverly using the empty ore hoppers to move coal from Utah and Colorado to Illinois in a back-haul arrangement, SP was able to maximize its use of equipment. Initially, new SP DASH 9s were standard power for these runs. Since SP power often ran through with the trains from terminal to terminal, SP's DASH 9-44CWs were regular visitors on the Wisconsin Central. In 1995, when SP took delivery of

even more modern AC4400CWs from General Electric, its DASH 9s were reassigned to other services and regularly used on the Sunset Route.

Although General Electric introduced its AC traction line just a year after the DASH 9, the line did not supersede the market for traditional DC traction locomotives. Several lines, such as Burlington Northern Santa Fe and Norfolk Southern, prefer DASH 9s to GE AC models, and their DASH 9s are built right alongside ACs at Building 10. What may be confusing to the casual observer are the external similarities between GE's DASH 9 and AC4400CW lines. In nearly all respects, these machines, despite their significantly different traction systems, have nearly the same external appearance. The best tip-off for the AC4400 is its much larger box behind the cab on the fireman's side (righthand side when viewed head-on) of the locomotive that contains the AC's inverters.

On March 3, 1997, former Chicago & North Western DASH 9s lead a Union Pacific double-stack eastbound through Clover Creek Canyon, Nevada, on the old Los Angeles & Salt Lake Route. North Western's DASH 9s were fresh out of GE's Erie, Pennsylvania, facility when UP decided to acquire the line. *Brian Solomon*

19 Electro-Motive
SD70MAC

The SD70MAC was the first commercially built American diesel locomotive with AC traction motors; Burlington Northern's commitment to General Motors made the development commercially viable. On March 8, 1996, three Burlington Northern SD70MACs lift a Powder River coal train up Nebraska's Crawford Hill. T. S. Hoover

Three Burlington Northern SD70MACs in silhouette against the sunset wheel a unit coal train east through the fields of Lehman's Dairy Farm at Phillipsburg, Texas, on January 14, 1996. Traveling the rails of the Santa Fe's Galveston Subdivision, this train is returning from delivering coal to Houston Lighting & Power's W. A. Parrish generating station south of Houston. Prior to the use of SD70MACs, these heavy 14,000-ton trains required a minimum of five six-axle DC traction locomotives to conquer the up-and-down "hogback" grades of this central Texas mainline. *Tom Kline*

Burlington Northern Chairman Gerald Grinstein was quoted in the May 1994 issue of *TRAINS* magazine as saying, "[The SD70MAC] may very well represent the most dramatic step forward since diesel replaced steam." With such a bold assertion, the casual observer may well expect the SD70MAC to have the appearance of a radical new machine. Quite contrary, an SD70MAC looks just like other modern Electro-Motive diesels. So, what then is special about it?

Until 1994, all commercially built North American diesel-electric locomotives used conventional DC traction motors. DC traction was well understood, developed, and straightforward. Although DC traction was the prevalent traction technology, it has several inherent limitations to locomotive performance, and by the early 1990s, American locomotive builders had reached the zenith of DC traction technology. The railroads' desire for greater power and better motor reliability pushed the development of three-phase AC traction technology.

While the use of AC traction seems to have appeared in America rather suddenly, in reality, developmental work had been ongoing for two decades. General Motors had been experimenting with three-phase AC motors since the mid-1970s, and during the late 1980s and early 1990s built several prototype locomotives with a three-phase AC

Three Burlington Northern SD70MACs lead coal empties west of Edgemont, South Dakota, on May 26, 1995. Three SD70MACs were standard Powder River coal train power. *Brian Solomon*

Among the last locomotives delivered new to Conrail were 15 SD70MACs. These 4,000-horsepower machines wore the same paint livery as the larger and more powerful SD80MACs delivered in 1995 and 1996. Here, a pair of new SD70MACs rolls eastward along the Mohawk River at Hoffmans, east of Amsterdam, New York, on October 30, 1998. *Brian Solomon*

afforded by three 4,000-horsepower SD70MACs could effectively do the same work as five 3,000-horsepower SD40-2s or C30-7s.

The SD70MAC's greatest strength is at starting and lower speeds. Where an SD40-2 produces just 87,150 pounds of continuous tractive effort, an SD80MAC can develop 137,000 pounds. Unlike conventional DC traction diesels like the SD40-2s, which are greatly limited at low speeds by the short time ratings imposed on DC motors to keep them from overheating, three-phase AC motors can operate at full power at slow speed indefinitely without risk of motor damage. This allows an SD70MAC to maintain very high tractive effort much longer than DC locomotives. An SD70MAC can produce greater tractive effort because of greater adhesion afforded through superior motor control and advanced wheel-slip systems. EMD and BN calculate tractive effort for an SD40-2 based on a 21 percent factor of adhesion, while a figure of between 33 and 38 percent adhesion is used (depending on rail conditions) for the SD70MAC. Banks of inverters convert direct current to simulated three-phase AC current for use by the traction motors. Modulating current frequency using sophisticated electronic controls regulates speed.

In addition to greater tractive effort, AC traction motors offer other important advantages over conventional DC traction, including more effective dynamic braking and longer motor life. These advantages reduce operational costs and potentially save money. But the savings have a price. An SD70MAC costs about 25 percent per unit more than a comparable EMD DC traction locomotive. For this reason, AC traction is not necessarily the best option in all situations. A railroad needs to weigh greater unit cost against the savings provided by improved performance and lower maintenance. This comparison harks back to Grinstein's steam-diesel analogy, in which the greater costs and efficiencies of early diesels outweighed the lower per-unit price of traditional steam locomotives. However, the cost savings of AC over DC compared with diesel to steam savings are neither as dramatic nor as universally true for all types of traffic.

Initially, BN ordered 350 SD70MACs, the first of which were delivered in December 1993. The type made its public debut in Fort Worth, Texas, on January 10, 1994, in a ceremony attended by top representatives of Burlington Northern, EMD, and Siemens AG. The success of the SD70MAC led BN and its successor, Burlington Northern Santa Fe (BNSF), to place large repeat orders for the locomotive. CSX and Conrail also received SD70MACs, although their fleets are much smaller than BNSF's. With the breakup of Conrail in 1999, all of that railroad's SD70MACs went to CSX.

Since mixing AC and DC traction locomotives diminishes the advantages of using AC traction, Burlington Northern Santa Fe has made a concerted effort to keep its SD70MACs in matched sets for dedicated service. While BNSF's SD70MACs were primarily purchased for coal service, they are also regularly used for moving other

traction system developed by the German electric firm Siemens AG. German engineers had refined AC traction for use on the Class 120 electric locomotive in the late 1970s, and later applied AC traction to the German high-speed passenger train known as the *InterCity Express* (ICE). In the mid-1980s, AC traction had also been developed for both French and Japanese high-speed trains, while AC traction diesels were developed for freight and passenger services in Scandinavia. The refinement of AC technology required a substantial developmental investment. By placing a very large order for hundreds of AC diesels, Burlington Northern provided EMD with the commitment it needed to refine a practical AC traction diesel-electric to haul its Powder River coal traffic.

In the 1970s, Burlington Northern (BN) had developed Wyoming's Powder River basin by building new lines into the region to move coal. Powder River coal is relatively close to the surface and therefore easy to mine. The coal is especially desirable because of its low sulfur content, which complies with modern environmental and pollution regulations. By the early 1990s, 30 percent of BN's traffic base came from coal, and the traffic was still growing. However, BN's traditional fleet of coal service locomotives, EMD SD40-2s and GE C30-7s, were approaching retirement. AC traction promised significantly greater tractive effort that would allow BN to use fewer locomotives to move equivalent tonnage. Specifically, superior adhesion bulk commodities like unit grain trains and iron ore trains. At times when coal traffic is down, BNSF has been known to occasionally assign SD70MACs to merchandise freight.

Brian Burns was a locomotive engineer for BNSF working out of Galesburg, Illinois, a division point located at a crucial junction of former Burlington and Santa Fe routes. Running east from Galesburg to Chicago are two double-track mainlines. The former Santa Fe line runs to the south via Streator, Illinois, and primarily handles intermodal trains and fast merchandise freight. Powder River coal trains are routed east over the former Burlington line via Mendota and Aurora, Illinois. At the later point there is a junction with the former Burlington "C&I" (Aurora to Savanna, Illinois) mainline that carries traffic between the Twin Cities (Minneapolis and St. Paul) and Chicago. The line between Aurora and Chicago is a triple-track Centralized Traffic Control route with very heavy freight and passenger traffic. Chicago's Metra operates 29 to 30 round trips per day over the line, with an especially intensive service during rush hour. Burns would often take loaded unit coal trains eastward. These were especially heavy trains for which the SD70MAC was built. As Burns explains:

Loaded coal trains usually had 117 to 120 hoppers, the cars weighed about 143 tons each, making for a train of about 17,000 tons. Normally, we would have just two SD70MACs. These engines are good pullers, but just two didn't have enough horsepower to make much speed. Sometimes we were thrown a bonus, and we'd be assigned three 'MACs, then we had plenty of power. With longer trains [those with 126 cars], the SD70MACs would be arranged as DPUs [distributed power units—see section on AC4400CW]. [In these situations] just one unit was on the point, while the other was positioned at the back of the train to relieve stress on the drawbars.

Burns would regularly take coal trains to Chicago, a maze of track and junctions where heavy freight traffic mixed with a busy suburban passenger service has long made it one of the most railroad-intensive places in the United States. But, coal trains are fairly low priority when it comes to making it through the Chicago terminal area.

"If everything went perfectly it would be a short run [from Galesburg], just three or four hours over the road; but eight hours was a more normal run," Burns recalls. "Often, we would get held west of Aurora [Illinois] for the "Dinky Rush,"—what we called the commuter rush on the railroad, the little Metra trains being the "Dinkies." Sometimes we would sit on the main at Eola, east of Aurora, waiting for a [clear] signal. Coal trains have a variety of destinations, and we might bring the train to any number of interchange points depending on where it was going."

The SD70MAC uses modern desktop controls instead of a conventional engineer's control stand. *Brian Solomon*

One advantage of using AC traction is that fewer locomotives are required to move a train, therefore less horsepower per ton is required, which results in a fuel savings. So, while a train with less power will still make it over the railroad, it will not be able to move as quickly. With bulk commodities like coal, slightly slower transit times are tolerated because the commodities are not as time sensitive. Among the new features incorporated on the SD70MAC were computerized desktop locomotive controls that EMD calls Integrated Cab Electronics (ICE). Although some view this as an improvement over the conventional locomotive control stand, the ICE controls are not universally liked. Brian Burns' describes one problem with the braking system,

On the early [SD70MAC] models, the [brake] handles were overly sensitive. This was sometimes a problem when trying to slow a train. If I went to make just a small reduction in the train air, I might accidentally take too much air off and set up the brakes. On later models this seems to have been corrected. A display screen allowed us to set the target brake application, which avoided the problem. Running the 'MACs in DPU had its advantages and disadvantages, too. By having a locomotive at both ends of the train, the air sets up from both ends, and with a long coal train that really made a difference and we could stop

much faster. On the downside, there were more instances of "kickers" [a flaw in the air line that causes an unintended emergency airbrake application that stops the train]. The 'MACs also have very powerful dynamic brakes which help to stop a heavy train.

The SD70MACs could best demonstrate their abilities to pull on heavy grades. While much has been made of the SD70MACs on Nebraska's Crawford Hill and crossing the Palmer Divide south of Denver, they have proven their merit on other grades as well. Former Conrail engineer Don Jilson tells of running a pair of SD70MACs with a coal train up New York's Attica Hill. Once, he picked up a heavy unit coal train at William Street in Buffalo, New York, that was destined for New York State Electric & Gas (which has powerplants at Dresden and Johnson City). Normally, if a heavy coal train came in from the west with a pair of SD40-2s or SD50s, a locomotive or two would be added at Buffalo, for the run over Attica and across the Southern Tier. Traditionally, engineers had rules of thumb for estimating their speed with heavy trains.

Jilson explains, "With DC traction [locomotives], rolling east of Buffalo, your speed at Sandwich Road in Marilla would be twice your speed up over Attica Hill." Since AC traction changes the whole power equation, Jilson wondered what would happen on the grade with two SD70MACs and about 110 cars of coal weighing an estimated 13,000 tons. As it happens, as he approached CP Attica [CP stands for "control

Above: Although three SD70MACs can produce 12,000 horsepower and more than 310,000 pounds tractive effort, helpers are still required on the sinuous crossing of Crawford Hill in western Nebraska. A pair of new SD70MACs shoves on the back of a coal train east of Crawford. *Brian Solomon*

Right: Wet rails reduce tractive effort, making it more difficult for locomotives to do their work. On this very wet day at Crawford Hill, three SD70MACs shove on the rear of a long coal train, while another three pull at the head end. While this train crawls upgrade at about 5 miles per hour, modern wheel-slip systems will keep it from stalling. *Brian Solomon*

point," a dispatcher-controlled switch] he was forced to slow his train to a near stop due to an awkward signaling arrangement at Attica. The dispatcher lined the coal train onto the siding at Attica, which resulted in the train running on the slower track up the grade. Attica has a sag at the base of the grade and having slowed to take the switch meant that Jilson lost most of his momentum. As the train climbed Attica Hill, it gradually lost speed and the two SD70MACs were reduced to a crawl by the grade. "At one point the train was moving at just 0.01 mile per hour!"

Jilson marvels. "But we didn't stall, and it took us 90 minutes to get through the 4- to 5-mile-long siding."

This ability to keep pulling, even at very slow speeds, is a key selling point of AC power. The Conrail coal train didn't make it over the road with great speed, but it also did not need a helper or extra locomotives. Using the SD70MACs, Conrail needed only two locomotives to move the train, instead of three or four—and in the end, the coal made its destination.

Burlington Northern Santa Fe was the result of a 1995 merger between Santa Fe and BN. The BNSF continues to assign SD70MACs to coal service, but has applied its own livery to the type. A pair of BNSF SD70MACs is seen at Palmer Lake, Colorado, in June 2000. The lead locomotive wears BNSF's latest livery, while the second unit is in the old BN executive scheme. *Michael L. Gardner*

20 General Electric AC4400CW

Southern Pacific AC4400CW 106 leads a loaded coal train into Minturn, Colorado. East of Minturn, the train will run with nine ACs arranged in sets of three. Two sets of manned helpers were needed to lift heavy trains over Tennessee Pass, the highest mainline grade in the United States. Brian Solomon

The sun sets over Colorado's Front Range as a Union Pacific AC4400CW leads a loaded coal train eastbound on the Kansas Pacific a few miles east of Denver. Union Pacific prefers General Electric AC traction diesels for coal service. *Brian Solomon*

On a cloudless morning in the Colorado Rockies during late summer 1995, the thin and clear mountain air reverberates with the low bass of distant diesel exhaust. The sun rises over Tennessee Pass, gracing the aspens that are just taking on their autumnal yellow hue. Slowly, ever so slowly, the diesel roar grows louder. The source of this noise is a heavily laden coal train, weighing more than 11,000 tons, that's slowly crawling its way up the former Denver & Rio Grande Western and presently climbing past Pando. Leading the train are three brand-new General Electric AC4400CWs wearing Southern Pacific's attractive gray and scarlet livery. Buried mid-train are two sets of manned helpers, each with three AC4400CWs; that's a total of nine big GEs, and they are producing an estimated 1,305,000 pounds of tractive effort. Train speed is a steady 6 miles per hour. With their sanders going and all locomotives in Run 8, the coal train grinds up past the Deene Tunnel, and in a little while reaches the top of this grueling 3 percent grade at the Tennessee Pass summit tunnel, more than 10,000 feet above sea level.

This was one of the most intense dramas modern railroading had to offer, but its stage presence was a short one. Southern Pacific received its first General Electric AC4400CWs a little more than a year before the company was acquired by Union Pacific. In fact, as this coal train ascended Tennessee Pass, the SP-UP merger negotiations were already underway. Following the merger, the route would be closed to through traffic. But this picture would start to change even sooner— the use of AC4400CWs as manned helpers on Tennessee Pass was cut short by modern technology implemented during the final months of

Southern Pacific operation. By 1996, SP was using AC4400CWs as radio-controlled remote helpers featuring GE-Harris Locotrol III technology. With Locotrol, a lead locomotive engineer can operate remote helpers from the head-end. This practice is described in industry terminology as "distributed power unit" operation, with the remote helpers known as DPUs.

Southern Pacific was absorbed by Union Pacific in late 1996 and Tennessee Pass closed less than a year later, but the state-of-the-art locomotive technology briefly deployed here has since became standard

Southern Pacific assigned its newest and most powerful locomotives to iron ore trains that were jointly run with Wisconsin Central. On April 6, 1996, a new AC4400CW, with a heavily laden train of taconite from Minnesota's Iron Range, pauses on the WC at Subway Road in North Fond du Lac, Wisconsin. *Brian Solomon*

Southern Pacific AC4400CWs descend Colorado's Tennessee Pass near Malta on July 21, 1995. Views like this one of modern SP power on Tennessee Pass were short-lived. Once Union Pacific took control of Southern Pacific, it was quick to close this high-altitude mountain line in favor of other routes. *Brian Solomon*

across the Union Pacific system. Furthermore, the AC4400CW is one of General Electric's most successful modern locomotives: by the year 2001, more than 1,800 had been built for North American operations.

General Electric followed General Motors' Electro-Motive Division in the development of AC traction diesel locomotives for heavy freight service. There are many parallels in the comparison of the development of EMD's SD70MAC for Burlington Northern's coal service and GE's development of the AC4400CW for CSX. Like BN, CSX moved a large amount of coal in heavily graded territory and was looking for a more economical locomotive fleet. High tractive effort, as well as other efficiencies afforded by AC traction, made this new technology especially appealing. When CSX committed to a large purchase, GE went ahead to develop the locomotive. SP was quick to follow CSX with a large order for the new ACs.

General Electric used a different approach in the development of AC locomotives than EMD. Whereas EMD, teamed up with the German firm Siemens to develop an AC traction system, General Electric had already pioneered modern AC traction technology for passenger rail and transit applications—it was just a matter of adapting its existing technology to a heavy diesel locomotive application.

The two primary differences between General Electric's AC traction system and EMD's are the inverters, banks of high-tech electrical equipment that convert direct current to a form of three-phase alternating current for traction. As explained in the section on SD70MACs, control of AC traction motors is accomplished through frequency modulation of the AC current, and advances in semiconductor technology had permitted the development of practical frequency control equipment. General Electric's later entry into the AC

Working with AC Traction: One Engineer's View

By John Gruber

Ron Morales, a Canadian Pacific engineer who operates GE AC4400s and EMD SD90MACs on a 173-mile run in Wisconsin and Illinois, doesn't like sitting at the new locomotive desks 8 to 12 hours a day. A traditional railroader, he readily talks about his preference for the old-style control stand and air gauges.

"If you are in an office, and at a desk long enough, you want to elevate your feet to relieve stress. You can do that with an SD40/60 or GP40—there is a heater in front of you—but not with the newer engines. Both the AC4400s and SD90MACs have desks with throttle and brake controls for the engineer. Imagine sitting for a day at a desk with a chair with limited movement," says Morales, an engineer since 1978.

"I saw one new engine with an older control stand at the Indiana Harbor Belt diesel house. It was a [modern] Canadian National [General Electric] engine, [but] with the old-style brake stand, air gauges, and controls. I thought, this is nice." But he is pleased that the newest group of AC4400s, delivered to CP in the fall of 2001, had air conditioning installed as standard equipment for the first time.

When Morales hired out as a hostler-helper on the Milwaukee Road in August 1966, his first engines were F7s, E7s, E8s, E9s, Fairbanks-Morse switch engines, Alco SWs, and an occasional Erie-built C Liner. He made the progression through hostler, yard fireman, yard engineer, road fireman, and finally road engineer

12 years after hiring out. He has seen the changes from Milwaukee Road to Soo Line and now Canadian Pacific.

A modern locomotive can handle a lot more tonnage. "CP is running many one-engine, 100-car trains. I call them 'one-engine wonders,' but they say they want to get their money's worth out of them. 'Why use two when one will do the job?' It takes you longer to get there, but the railroad somehow figures the economics is there and it's more productive to run one-engine trains."

The new locomotives do the job for the railroad. "These are the tools they give us, that is what we work with," he continues. "The GE is a heavy-haul engine. It takes awhile to build up the tractive effort, which translates to pulling power, so it takes awhile for a GE to get up to speed. If you have two, you get up there quicker than one, obviously."

Morales works the "PB" pool (Portage, Wisconsin, to Bensenville Yard, Chicago, Illinois). Chicago, he likes to point out, is still the railroad capital of the world, and he enjoys the challenge of running trains into "Railcity, U.S.A."

How long the trip takes depends on what kind of train he is on. "The Expediters, our hotshots, are allowed 60 miles per hour. I have had runs where 3 hours and 25 minutes after we departed Bensenville, the conductor and myself arrived in Portage, or 3 hours and 40 minutes after departing Bensenville we were in Portage via Tower A5. Trips like these are rare; it all depends on the dispatchers, clear signals, good power, or a short train. I have worked 12 hours–plus many times, the 'plus' being an arbitrary called tow-in, because we are not allowed to perform service after 12 hours. It still might

take you an hour or two to get from the parked engine or train to the hotel to get our rest. That hour or two is tow-in time."

Computers do a lot of the internal work, but the locomotive engineer still controls what happens in the cab, Morales explains. "The engineer cracks the throttle; applies or releases the train and engine brakes; regulates the dynamic brake; blows the horn; rings the bell; adjusts the headlights; reads the orders; gets supplies; inspects and repairs when needed the one or more engines in his charge; calls out and complies with signal indications, flags, fuses, and signs; must be aware of temporary and permanent speed restrictions, timetables, or special instructions including foreign railroads he is required to run on, or any hazardous material restrictions; and, finally, must have knowledge and obedience to all safety and General Code of Operating Rules, because every trip is a test of our abilities to perform our job safely, while being on call 24 hours a day 7 days a week.

"Yes, computer chips do handle some internal engine controls and some parts of the air brake system, but the locomotive engineer is the one who makes the initial judgment on when and where to stop a train, or how fast it speeds up or slows down. The computers just follow through on his or her judgment and decisions, based on training, experience, train makeup, tonnage, speed, weather conditions, and track profile, along with many other factors."

Morales obviously likes the work. He likes the powerful, modern, air-conditioned locomotives, but fondly speaks of the traditional, hands-on control stands so much a part of his earlier years on the railroad.

General Electric's AC4400CW and DASH 9s both feature the GE Hi-Ad truck. This was designed for high adhesion to provide greater tractive effort than earlier truck designs. *Brian Solomon*

locomotive market encouraged the company to innovate in order to secure a market advantage. While the EMD-Siemens AC control system uses two inverters—one for each truck, or one per three motors—General Electric's system uses six inverters, assigning one to each traction motor. This allows for individual axle control, permitting higher tractive effort and affording greater reliability. An EMD locomotive would have to reduce power to three axles to prevent wheel slip, while a GE can regulate power to each axle.

GE's system also allows for greater variance in wheel diameter, offering a maintenance advantage. The six-inverter system's distinct reliability advantage is simple. A single inverter failure on an SD70MAC can cut locomotive output by as much as 50 percent. However with GE, a single inverter failure will result in just a 12 percent tractive effort loss (the inverters have sufficient capacity to absorb some of the power loss caused by a single failure). However, in most

situations, a single inverter failure on a GE will not result in an appreciable change in horsepower because the remaining inverters can make up the output difference.

Another design distinction between EMD and GE inverters is the method of cooling. Where EMD uses a chemical cooling system to disperse the intense heat generated by the inverters, General Electric uses an air-cooling system. The latter is less harmful to the environment, requires less maintenance, and is therefore more economical for the user.

The development of the AC4400CW provided General Electric a valuable product with which to expand its customer base. In addition to securing large orders from existing customers such as CSX and Union Pacific, GE was also able to attract its first order for road diesels from Canadian Pacific and Kansas City Southern, both longstanding EMD customers. GE has also sold ACs to recently privatized Mexican railways.

On December 10, 1997, Canadian Pacific AC4400CW 9492 leads an eastbound coal train across the massive bridge at Lethbridge, Alberta. Notice the mid-train distributed power units (radio-controlled helpers) working toward the back of the train. *Eric T. Hendrickson*

Overleaf: The Powder River Basin in eastern Wyoming is the location of dozens of coal mines. The market for Powder River coal has boomed since the area was first developed by Burlington Northern in the 1970s. Today, the area is served by BNSF and Union Pacific and between the two lines as many as 60 heavy coal trains are moved daily. Since coal traffic and AC traction go hand in hand, the Powder River Basin is a great place to see modern AC locomotives in action. *Tim Doherty and Tom Mangan*

Above: From the front end, the AC4400CW is virtually indistinguishable from GE's DC traction locomotives. On SP, a good spotting feature was the spacing between the letters on the nose. The AC's were close together, as seen here, while the "S" and "P" were noticeably separated on SP's DC traction DASH 9-44CWs. *Brian Solomon*

Above right: Two CSX 500 Series AC4400CWs form the Burnsville Helper at Burnsville Junction, West Virginia. These locomotives will assist the next Cowen-to-Grafton coal drag on the former B&O Cowen Subdivision, October 23, 2001. *T. S. Hoover*

Not all AC4400CWs are the same. Since the model debuted in 1994, GE has continuously implemented design improvements aimed at better performance and increased reliability. Among those improvements have been the development of a "steerable" truck and the introduction of Sampled Axle Speed computer software in place of the older True Ground Speed Sensor (TGSS). The former system, as explained by Jay Potter in his article "Grafton's 500s" published in *Diesel Era*, is used to monitor the speed of individual axles and is a more reliable way of controlling wheel slip than using Doppler radar as employed by TGSS. Potter's article specifically highlights CSX's specialized AC4400CWs, known by CSX employees in West Virginia as "500s." These locomotives are some of the most modern GEs operating today. They are unusual in CSX's GE fleet because they have an extra 10 tons of ballast to boost their tractive effort, making them more effective in slow-speed mineral service on the old Baltimore & Ohio West End grades.

Above: A brand-new Kansas City Southern AC4400CW 2030 turns back on its train as it makes a giant U-turn through the small town of Blanchard, Louisiana, on September 29, 2000. Headed for the Southwest Electric Power Company's generating plant at Welsh, Texas, this westbound—KCS train 91—diverts off the north-south Shreveport Subdivision and onto the east-west Greenville Subdivision at Texas Junction on the edge of town. Once requiring four to five EMD locomotives with DC traction motors, this heavy train now needs just two of these 4,400-horsepower GEs with AC-driven motors. *Tom Kline*

Left: Canadian Pacific 9585 blasts through Canmore, Alberta, in the summer of 1998. Canadian Pacific has been buying General Electric AC4400CWs in large numbers since 1995. *Eric T. Hendrickson*

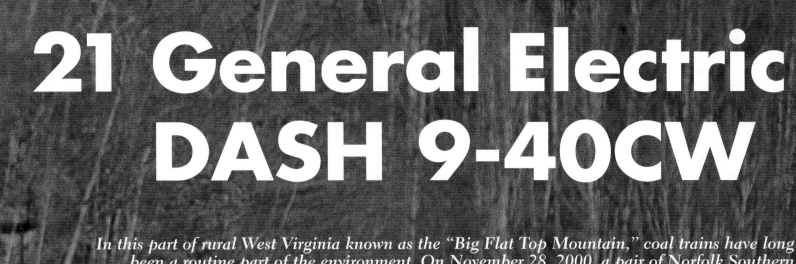

21 General Electric DASH 9-40CW

In this part of rural West Virginia known as the "Big Flat Top Mountain," coal trains have long been a routine part of the environment. On November 28, 2000, a pair of Norfolk Southern DASH 9-40CWs leads a heavy coal train at the Elkhorn Tunnel. A three-unit pusher is at the back shoving as hard as it can. T. S. Hoover

Norfolk Southern DASH 9-40CWs switch a salt train at Silver Springs, New York. Although NS DASH 9-40CWs have North American Safety Cabs, they feature traditional engineer control stands to make switching moves like this one easier to perform. *Brian Solomon*

The fundamental purpose of a locomotive design is to give a railroad the most cost-effective means of moving trains. There are many different railroads, each with different traffic and operating conditions, so there is no one locomotive that can best suit all railroads' needs all the time. In recent years, various models of modern high-horsepower, six-motor diesels have come to dominate North American railroads. Yet within this basic characterization there are distinct variations. Examining the motive power application of the four largest American railroad systems, we find four distinctly different motive power strategies for moving long freight trains: Union Pacific purchases General Motors DC traction six-motor diesels for general freight and intermodal services, while it acquires General Electric six-motor AC traction diesels for coal service. Burlington Northern Santa Fe has acquired GE six-motor DC units for general freight and intermodal, while using its large fleet of General Motors SD70MACs for coal service. CSX has been acquiring a large fleet of six-motor AC units, primarily from GE, for both general service and coal service, however it has specialized models of AC units tailored for specific services as described in the sections about General Electric's AC4400CW and AC6000CW. Norfolk Southern has not

embraced AC traction at all, instead favoring a more conservative approach. Since the mid-1990s the bulk of its locomotive acquisitions have been General Electric six-motor units, which it assigns to all types of heavy services rather than focusing on specialized locomotive fleets. The basic building block of the NS fleet is General Electric's DASH 9-40CW, a 4,000-horsepower DC traction locomotive model that, as of this writing in 2002, is only utilized by NS.

Norfolk Southern has set ideas on what it wants and needs, and is not willing to pay for qualities that it doesn't believe will benefit its operations. This tradition goes back a long way. Following World War II, NS predecessor Norfolk & Western had a different business strategy than most other railroads, and the company's large coal reserves made it especially advantageous for it to stick with steam power despite the perceived advantages of the new diesels. Rather than purchase fleets of EMD F7s or Alco FAs, it continued to perfect its own steam designs. As a result, N&W was the last major railroad to build and operate steam locomotives in the United States. In more modern times, Norfolk Southern has viewed motive power innovations in a similar light. Although other lines found advantages to North American Safety Cab, NS continued to specify conventional cabs. Despite the trend toward AC traction for heavy drag service, NS has chosen to stick with DC traction. While other North American lines were ordering diesels in the 4,400- to 6,000-horsepower range, NS has been content to order locomotives with a more nominal figure. NS has not determined that these features provide added value, and thus has not been willing to pay extra for them. When it began ordering new DASH 9s from GE in 1995, it requested that the maximum output be limited to just 4,000 horsepower.

Norfolk Southern finds that a 4,000-horsepower locomotive provides just the right amount of power for the job it's assigned to do. In the highest throttle notch, a 4,400-horsepower locomotive will burn more fuel than a 4,000-horsepower locomotive. In other words, NS sees a 4,400-horsepower locomotive as an unnecessary use of resources. Over the course of several years, lower fuel consumption multiplied by hundreds of locomotives adds up to considerable savings.

Norfolk Southern's first DASH 9s featured conventional cabs—the only DASH 9s so built—while later NS DASH 9s were built with Safety Cabs. The change in cab style reflected a change in the cost structure; when the Safety Cab was first introduced as an option, locomotives with the design cost more than comparable machines with conventional cabs. By the mid-1990s the situation had reversed. The wide-nose North American Safety Cab design had become a standard feature for new General Electric locomotives while the conventional cab was now a specialty option.

NS' wide-cab DASH 9s were still built with conventional control stands rather than more modern electronic desktop controls. One advantage of the conventional arrangement is that locomotive engineers can more easily operate the locomotive in both directions,

The General Electric DASH 9 has become NS' standard modern road locomotive. These machines are used in all kinds of road service, from heavy coal drags to priority intermodal runs. On September 30, 2000, a westbound intermodal train passes the (now-closed) MG tower on the former Pennsylvania Railroad mainline west of Horse Shoe Curve. *Brian Solomon*

unlike desktop controls, which make reverse running awkward. And since NS often requires road locomotives to make switching moves, it is advantageous for locomotive engineers to be able to run comfortably in both directions.

Mechanically speaking, Norfolk Southern's DASH 9-40CWs are basically the same as General Electric's standard DASH 9-44CW. They use the same frame, high-adhesion trucks, 16-cylinder 7-FDL engine, and 752AH-31 traction motors. What makes them different is the software strategy in the engine's governing unit (abbreviated "EGU," the onboard computer that runs the diesel engine). On Norfolk Southern's DASH 9-40CWs, the EGU limits maximum output in Run 8 to save fuel. There is no difference in output in the lower throttle positions. A key-operated switch reverts the EGU strategy for the highest throttle position to the standard 4,400-horsepower maximum output. This feature allows NS management to alter the top performance characteristics of individual locomotives when higher output is desired. In this way, NS can carefully control fuel consumption by limiting when the maximum throttle output is used.

Most of the time, NS' DASH 9s are run in the 4,000-horsepower mode, which seems to suit NS operations satisfactorily. Norfolk Southern's system of assigning locomotives is different from most American railroads. In most applications, NS assigns locomotives to trains based on the number of axles rather than the horsepower-per-ton basis that is more common in the industry. Norfolk Southern's system doesn't prejudice locomotive assignments by the rated output of individual locomotive types, however, NS does make a distinction between high-adhesion locomotives like the DASH 9s and traditional locomotives with normal adhesion characteristics. Since high-adhesion locomotives are capable of pulling more than normal-adhesion machines, NS treats them as having an additional axle. The flexibility of the NS fleet is one of the goals behind its axle-based assignment system. Its GE DASH 9s can be assigned to all types of road freights. The theory is NS doesn't need a specialized fleet for coal service and another general freight service like UP and BNSF do. So a DASH 9 that worked on a unit coal train up the Elkhorn Grade one day, may be assigned to a priority intermodal freight the next. This arrangement is intended to allow NS to better utilize its fleet. Savings are achieved through better fleet

Norfolk Southern's early DASH 9s featured traditional cabs instead of North American Safety Cabs. These locomotives were the only DASH 9s built this way and carry the designation DASH 9-40C. *Brian Solomon*

Norfolk Southern rates locomotives differently than most other railroads. It has six categories of locomotive. DASH 9s, along with other very modern six-motor locomotives, are considered "High Adhesion" and are assigned accordingly. Here, a DASH 9-40CW and an SD60 lead an empty coal hopper train at CP Stoney on the Buffalo Line north of Harrisburg, Pennsylvania. *Brian Solomon*

management and reduced maintenance costs afforded by a simplified parts supply and common maintenance practices for all locomotives.

One of the most difficult jobs NS assigns to its DASH 9s is moving loaded eastbound unit coal trains up the former Norfolk & Western Elkhorn Grade in rural West Virginia. The old N&W has a rich history moving coal. It was made famous for its late-era steam operations, which were beautifully captured in the night photographs crafted by master photographer O. Winston Link in the 1950s. The west slope of the Elkhorn Grade is known for its challenging operations. Although a line relocation in 1950 reduced the gradient and

curvature and provided a ventilated double-track tunnel, the Elkhorn is still a tough pull that requires heavy trains to operate with pushers. The ruling grade is 1.4 percent, which will slow a heavily laden train to just 8 miles per hour. Unlike other coal lines that use radio-controlled distributed power (remote-controlled helpers), NS continues to rely on conventional manned helpers, which are known as "pushers."

In a typical run, two DASH 9s may be assigned to a 15,000-ton coal train that begins its run from the yard at Williamson, West Virginia. Heading east, the train starts up a nominal grade to a location known on the railroad as "Farm." Here, the dispatcher instructs

the head-end crew to hold on the mainline. A three-unit DASH 9 pusher drops down the grade past the loaded train and crosses from one track to the other at Mohegan. Once crossed over, the pusher reverses direction and comes up against the back of the coal train. This is an age-old tradition—pushers have been tying on to the back of coal trains at Farm since the steam days. Today this is made easier by a specialized electrically controlled device that sits on the handrails of the lead pusher. Known as the "helper link box," this device allows the engineer to remotely pull the coupler pin on the pusher from the engine cab. Not only does this save time, it reduces the labor of cutting manned pushers on to a train and permits the pusher to cut out on the fly, saving time. After the pushers are coupled to the coal train, the head-end engineer and pusher engineer compare airbrake information and the train is ready to continue its ascent of the Elkhorn Grade. The pusher engineer starts moving first, announcing over the radio, "I'm coming up against you." This reduces the amount of slack between the cars in the train, which makes it easier for the head end to get started. The head-end engineer listens for the slack running in, releases the independent brakes on the engines, and begins to notch up the engine. Typically, the pushers will be shoving as hard as they

can while the head end maintains the speed of the train. As the train climbs the grade, the head-end engineer calls out signal aspects over the radio, which are then echoed in acknowledgment by the pusher engineer. Each signal has a name.

"Clear Kimball!"

"Clear Kimball." Replies the pusher. (Incidentally, Kimball is a town on the Elkhorn Grade named for one of N&W's first presidents.)

A Norfolk Southern DASH 9-40C leads an intermodal train eastbound on the westbound main track on the old Erie Railroad at Endicott, New York, in October 2001. The train passes the very last operational Union Switch & Signal semaphore on this line, and one of the few remaining semaphores left in the United States. *Brian Solomon*

So long as the road ahead is clear, the pusher can keep shoving hard in Run 8. If the signals start to display more restrictive aspects, the pusher may need to notch back. The grade is the toughest east of Northfork, and here the locomotives work their hardest. After exiting the new Elkhorn Tunnel, the railroad dips into a short downgrade, described as a "sag," then passes though a yard at Flat Top. Some coal trains pause here to remove their pushers, but this train consists of tidewater-bound export coal and will keep its pusher all the way to Bluefield.

Yarding a heavily loaded train at Bluefield is tricky business because the yard is located right at a summit. The grade descends in both directions from here. So once the lead locomotives are over the hump and started into the downgrade, the head-end engineer must reduce power and ease the train to a stop while the pusher still shoves hard on the back of the train. If the pusher eases off too soon,

the weight of the train will cause the pushers to stall while they are still trying to push forward. This situation can be serious, for if the situation is not rectified, gravity takes over and the train will force the pushers back down the grade while the motors are still trying to move forward. This causes a condition known as "plugging the motors," an industry term describing an instance in which gravity overcomes the forward motion of the motors and puts unusually high stress on mechanical and electrical components. It can be extremely damaging to the equipment.

East of Bluefield, the train faces the Whitethorn Grade. Here, another pair of DASH 9s assists from Whitethorn to Merrimack. The daily drama of lifting trains over the Elkhorn Grade, once the domain of N&W's famous Y6-class Mallets, is now the charge of its six-motor General Electric locomotives.

Above: Coming down the "Slide." DASH 9s ease a long intermodal train down the especially steep grade east of the New Portage Tunnel in Gallitzin, Pennsylvania, on September 30, 2000. *Brian Solomon*

Left: DASH 9s lead a Norfolk Southern RoadRailer eastbound at South Fork, Pennsylvania, in March 2001. *Brian Solomon*

22 Electro-Motive SD80MAC

Conrail's SD80MACs were the only locomotives to use a 20-cylinder 710G3B prime mover. These powerful machines were rated at 5,000 horsepower and normally operated in pairs. Conrail SD80MAC 4124 waits at Palmer, Massachusetts, on November 23, 1996, for an eastbound train to pass. Brian Solomon

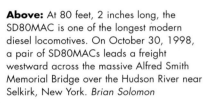

In the larger scheme of locomotive history, the SD80MAC is an anomaly in modern locomotive practice. The type was neither especially numerous nor did it make a significant influence on further development. However, the SD80MAC is a distinctive modern type that generated considerable interest when it was new.

In 1995, on the heels of Burlington Northern's large order for SD70MACs, Conrail ordered a small fleet of similar AC traction locomotives from the Electro-Motive Division. Instead of the common 16-cylinder 710G engine, the prime mover used by many modern EMD locomotives, the SD80MAC employs a 20-cylinder 710. Although there was no railway precedent for this big engine, the 20-cylinder 710G was not unknown and had been employed in marine applications. The larger engine produced 20 percent more power than the 16-cylinder 710G, allowing EMD to build a 5,000-horsepower locomotive—the most powerful of any on the market at that time. While EMD was developing its entirely new H-Engine—a design intended to produce 6,000-horsepower for use in its SD90MAC—at the time the SD80MAC was built, the new engine was just in the developmental stage and not expected to be ready for several years to come. By contrast, the 20-cylinder 710 was available immediately.

Electro-Motive Division built 28 SD80MACs for Conrail between 1995 and 1996. (Conrail later acquired two SD80MAC demos, bringing their fleet to 30 units.) These were by far the largest and most powerful locomotives to serve the railroad. Each measured 80 feet, 2 inches long, weighed approximately 430,000 pounds fully serviceable, and could produce 185,000 pounds starting tractive effort. Through the use of advanced wheel-slip control afforded by AC traction technology and

microprocessors, a pair of SD80MACs rated at 10,000 horsepower was designed to replace four DC traction locomotives with a combined 12,000 horsepower in like service. Two SD80MACs produce less horsepower than do four of the older locomotives, but they have equivalent tractive effort.

While the performance of the SD70MAC has been compared with the SD40-2, the proper comparison for the SD80MAC is not EMD's SD40-2, but General Electric's C30-7As. Conrail had 50 of the later locomotives, which it routinely assigned to trains running on its heavily graded Boston & Albany route. Unlike conventional C30-7s that employed a 16-cylinder FDL engine, the C30-7A used a 12-cylinder FDL and was designed for fuel-efficient operation in a high-tractive-effort application. Each locomotive developed 3,000 horsepower and could produce 120,000 pounds starting tractive effort and 96,900 pounds continuous tractive effort. While four GEs could produce slightly greater starting force than two SD80MACs, they could only maintain it for a short time. Conrail had routinely assigned its C30-7As and experimental C32-8s to heavy freight service on the B&A. A set of four GEs could easily lift 8,000 tons eastbound over the B&A.

A more difficult task was hauling heavy westbound trains. The toughest grade on the B&A is the east slope of Washington Hill in the Berkshires, which has a ruling grade of 1.67 percent. What makes the line difficult is its combination of a prolonged grade with numerous reverse curves. In the Conrail era, westbound trains were limited to 7,500 tons without a helper. Helper operations had been standard practice in the steam era and continued until 1982, at which time they were discontinued as a cost-saving measure.

With the breakup of Conrail in 1999, Norfolk Southern inherited 17 SD80MACs. These locomotives are an "orphan" AC traction fleet, as NS is otherwise all DC traction. This makes them unusual for two reasons: in addition to being ACs, they are also the only 20-cylinder locomotives on NS. In March 2001, NS SD80MAC 7213 works the helper on an empty coal train at South Fork, Pennsylvania, that is destined for Central City by way of a branchline that diverges from the old Pennsylvania mainline here. *Brian Solomon*

Traditionally, helpers operated over Washington Hill between Chester, Massachusetts, to Hinsdale or Pittsfield. The balance of traffic over the B&A favors eastbound traffic; thus, generally speaking, westbound trains climbing Washington Hill weigh less than their westbound counterparts.

There are several exceptions to this pattern. In 1990, paper and timber traffic from northern New England that traditionally moved over the Boston & Maine route via the Hoosac Tunnel was shifted to the Worcester, Massachusetts, interchange and run west over the B&A. This traffic is heavy and often runs in fully loaded trains. Also, heavy ballast trains originating at Traprock in West Springfield, Massachusetts, for points west of Selkirk, New York, would test the ability of any locomotive. If everything was functioning perfectly, ballast trains crawled up the mountain. However, if a train was underpowered, or if locomotives were not loaded properly, a heavy train would grind to a halt near Milepost 129. Rain and snow further reduce tractive effort, and many a westbound has stalled ascending the Berkshires on a wet day.

The challenge for the SD80MAC was to bring the heaviest trains upgrade using less power than any other locomotive. On many days they met this challenge, but sometimes they failed, too. In their early days on Conrail in 1995 and 1996, the SD80MACs suffered from reliability issues, which has been attributed in part to crews becoming accustomed to the differences in operation between AC traction locomotives and traditional DC locomotives. The ability of an AC locomotive to keep pulling even at extremely slow speeds may not have been initially understood or accepted by some locomotive engineers. Former Conrail locomotive engineer Don Jilson says that to run an AC traction locomotive properly on a heavy grade you need to "just leave the throttle in run and let the locomotive do the work." He points out that with older DC traction, an engineer needs to throttle down manually if the locomotive loses traction, but with modern ACs the computer automatically compensates for each axle individually. This allows an AC locomotive to maintain maximum power while minimizing the effects of slip. Climbing Washington Hill, SD80MACs might be reduced to less than 1 mile per hour, but will still be able to make the grade. One difficulty with this philosophy is that SD80MACs did not power all trains on the B&A route. The slow-moving AC-powered train introduces capacity issues that may end up increasing costs rather than lowering them. While an AC-powered train slugging it out at Milepost 129 at 1 mile per hour will eventually make the summit, a conventional DC train following behind will not be able to make the grade at such speeds. At the very least, the following train may have to wait until the track ahead is clear. This slows the operation and results in poorer use of equipment and crews.

Between 1996 and 1999, roughly six pairs of SD80MACs daily worked the B&A route between Conrail's enormous yard at Selkirk, New York (located south of Albany), and Boston, hauling roughly half the trains moving over the B&A route, including the heavy ballast trains and some intermodal runs. When Conrail was split between Norfolk Southern and CSX in June 1999, so was the SD80MAC fleet. While CSX's SD80MACs still occasionally run on the B&A, they are no longer standard motive power on the line. Instead, CSX has assigned its more powerful General Electric AC6000CWs to the route.

A pair of glistening SD80MACs leads an eastbound freight at Washington, Massachusetts. Conrail applied a new paint scheme to its SD80MACs in order to make them easy to distinguish from DC traction locomotives. The only other locomotives to wear this livery were Conrail's small fleet of SD70MACs. *Brian Solomon*

23 General Electric AC6000CW

Since 2000, pairs of General Electric AC6000CWs have been standard motive power on the old Boston & Albany mainline. In the late Conrail era this route was a regular stomping ground for the 20-cylinder SD80MAC. Now, the throaty roar of GE's 7HDL16 can be heard climbing along the West Branch of Westfield River. In October 2001, a pair of AC6000CWs climbs west along Route 20 in Huntington, Massachusetts. Brian Solomon

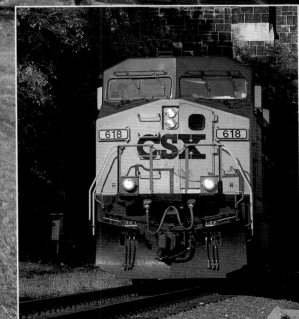

Right: A brand-new Union Pacific AC6000CW shines in the sun. Equipped with GE's new 7HDL16 engine, the AC6000CW is the most powerful single-engine diesel-electric built by GE to date. T. S. Hoover Far right: On Halloween Day 1999, CSX AC6000CW 618 exits the tunnel at West Point Tunnel, New York. Brian Solomon

Starting in 1995, General Electric delivered "convertible" AC6000CWs to Union Pacific. These locomotives featured the larger platform designed for the new 6,000-horsepower 7HDL16 engine, but were powered by GE's traditional 7FDL16 and rated at just 4,400 horsepower. Union Pacific 7026 looms out of the setting sun at Colo, Iowa, on the former Chicago & North Western mainline. *Brian Solomon*

Six thousand horsepower under a single hood is as much power as one can expect from any single diesel-electric locomotive on the rails today. That's a lot of power from one locomotive. In horsepower terms alone, it was equal to that produced by a four-unit A-B-B-A set of Alco FA-1s from the late 1940s, or a three-unit set of EMD GP20s from the early 1960s. More to the point, it equals the horsepower output of two EMD SD40-2s, GP40-2s, or General Electric C30-7s, each of which was rated at 3,000 horsepower. And horsepower is what the AC6000CW is all about—enough horsepower to effect a "one-for-two replacement of older DC locomotives," to quote General Electric promotional literature. General Electric has designed its most powerful diesel-electric for high-horsepower applications like high-speed long-distance intermodal services, instead of high-tractive-effort applications, such as moving heavy unit coal trains. The latter application is the domain of GE's AC4400CW, discussed previously. While the AC6000CW can be used in mineral service, such an application normally requires locomotives to lug at slow speeds and would not take full advantage of the unit's 6,000-horsepower potential.

Up until the AC6000CW, all General Electric road diesel locomotives had been powered by variants of the Cooper-Bessemer–designed 7FDL diesel engine. GE had satisfactorily reached the maximum output from the 7FDL at 4,400 horsepower, so to obtain 6,000 horsepower from a single powerplant, General Electric needed an entirely new engine. It worked with the German manufacturer Deutz MWM in the development of the 7HDL engine. Like GE's 7FDL, the new engine uses a four-cycle design in a 45-degree "V" arrangement. Each of its 16 cylinders has a 250x320-millimeter (9x10-1/2 inches) bore and stroke, operating at maximum 1,050 rpm. Other features include dual turbochargers (in place of the single large turbocharger used on earlier engines) and state-of-the-art electronic fuel injection. General Electric–advertised benefits of the 7HDL design include a faster load time than the 7FDL-16, more reliable components, ease of maintenance as a result of a more accessible design, and increased fuel efficiency.

General Electric, like General Motors, made the unusual move in the locomotive business by taking orders for 6,000-horsepower locomotives in advance of developing a working prototype. Prior to the commercial availability of the new 7HDL engine, GE built locomotives capable of carrying the big engine, complete with a 76-foot-long platform and larger radiators, but powered by the traditional 7FDL-16 engine, rated at just 4,400 horsepower.

One design feature that made this unusual arrangement possible was that both the AC4400CW and AC6000CW use the same electrical components. In 1996, having just absorbed Chicago & North Western, and in preparation for its merger with Southern Pacific, Union Pacific was in desperate need for new locomotives. For this reason, it accepted "convertible" machines both from GE and GM to bridge the gap in its fleet. There has been confusion as to what to call convertible locomotives. Since Union Pacific had not adopted GE's current designation system, as J. David Ingles reported in the November 1998 issue of *TRAINS*, to avoid undesirable mix-ups in its day-to-day operations, UP designated its big convertible GEs as C6044ACs, while conventional AC4400CWs are called C44ACs, and true AC6000CWs are designated C60ACs. Its EMDs are designated with a similar logic (see SD90MAC). Union Pacific assigned many of its C6044ACs to Powder River coal service.

The 7HDL-16 engine took longer to perfect than General Electric and the railroads initially anticipated, but by 1998 it was in regular production. Since that time, both Union Pacific and CSX have received production AC6000CWs. According to Jay Potter's detailed article, "Shoving with 12,000 Horsepower" (published in *Diesel Era*, Volume 9, Number 6), CSX tested its first AC6000CWs in helper service on the old Baltimore & Ohio West End grades in the Alleghenies between Keyser and Grafton, West Virginia. The locomotives performed well. Potter explains that with 166,000 pounds of tractive effort, CSX noted its AC6000CWs had "the highest tractive rating ever produced in a single-engine freight locomotive" (a statistic soon claimed by EMD's SD90MAC).

In 1999, CSX assumed operations of portions of the Conrail system, including much of the old New York Central east of Cleveland, Ohio. It is here that CSX has assigned many of its new AC6000CWs. The locomotives normally work in matched pairs on both intermodal and manifest trains. They can be seen running along the west bank of the Hudson on CSX's River Line heading to and from terminals in northern New Jersey, climbing the Boston & Albany grades in western Massachusetts, and running along the New York Central's famous Water Level Route west of Amsterdam, New York. Union Pacific's AC6000CW fleet rides on General Electric's modern high-adhesion trucks, while CSXs ride on GE's steerable trucks, which perform similarly to EMD's HTCR radial truck (see SD70M).

General Electric's AC6000CWs are not strictly for the North American market. GE has built a fleet of specialized AC6000CWs for mineral service on BHP Iron Ore in Australia. These machines are more heavily ballasted than American locomotives and designed for a very high-tractive-effort application.

Although dual cab diesels are common in much of the world, they have not enjoyed widespread application in the United States, mainly due to the high cost of locomotive cabs and the nature of locomotive assignments. In most applications, two or more locomotives are normally required, so using locomotives with dual cabs has no significant advantage. Some lines, such as Norfolk Southern, have ordered locomotives with dual controls for bi-directional operations, but a modern Safety Cab arrangement with desktop controls is not conducive to bi-directional operation. Appropriate turning facilities are no longer available at all terminals, and since applications like short, fast intermodal trains, for which a single AC6000CW would provide sufficient power, a dual-cab AC6000CW has been proposed, although as of this writing, none have been built.

Top: The high horsepower of an AC6000CW makes it ideal for intermodal work. A pair of AC6000CWs leads a CSX intermodal train from Boston, Massachusetts, off the Boston Line at CPSK in Selkirk, New York. In the distance, former Conrail DASH 8-40CWs are holding with an empty auto-rack train. *Brian Solomon*

Above: On a bright April 2001 morning, a pair of CSX AC6000CWs leads an eastbound intermodal train at Guilderland, New York. *Brian Solomon*

Left: On a clear October 2000 afternoon, CSX AC6000CWs accelerates westbound at CP 83 in Palmer, Massachusetts, with the Q423, a merchandise freight bound for Selkirk, New York. *Brian Solomon*

24 Electro-Motive SD90MAC

Like the SD80MAC, the SD90MAC is 80 feet, 2 inches long. An SD90MAC (SD9043AC) and AC4400CW pause at Woodbine, Iowa, on the former Chicago & North Western mainline to Omaha, Nebraska, and Council Bluffs, Iowa.
Brian Solomon

A pair of EMD SD90MACs and a General Electric AC6000CW lead a Powder River coal train. Union Pacific's 8000 to 8300 Series SD90MACs are powered by a 16-cylinder 710G engine and rated at just 4,300 horsepower. As a result, they are designated as SD9043AC by Union Pacific to indicate the lower output. Only the 8500 Series SD90MAC has the new engine rated at 6,000 horsepower. Tim Doherty

One development goal of AC traction was a single-engine 6,000-horsepower locomotive that would enable railroads to replace 3,000-horsepower locomotives on a one-for-two basis. This sort of strategy had worked effectively in the early 1960s, when locomotive builders introduced 3,000-horsepower second-generation models to allow the one-for-two replacement of postwar-era F-Units and similar locomotives. Building a single unit with a very high horsepower rating was not new to EMD. The company had built double-diesels in the 1960s with high-horsepower output. (As described earlier, the DDA40X was rated at 6,600 horsepower.) So what is so significant about the development of the 6,000-horsepower SD90MAC-H?

The DDA40X was a specialty product with limited application. Because of its enormous length and four-axle trucks, the DDA40X was not suited for general service on most lines. Furthermore, at the time the DDA40X was built, fuel-efficiency and emissions were secondary design concerns. Using modern three-phase AC traction technology and a state-of-the-art diesel engine design, the SD90MAC-H was intended as a fuel-efficient and powerful motive power solution for modern freight railroads.

The SD90MAC-H uses most of the same equipment as EMD's 5,000-horsepower SD80MAC, including an 80-foot-2-inch platform, HTCR II radial (self-steering) trucks with 45-inch wheels, a modern WhisperCab, and enormous angled radiators at the rear of the locomotive. As a result, the two machines look nearly identical. The significant defining feature of the SD90MAC-H is EMD's specially designed H-Engine, model designation GM16V265. Unlike previous EMD engines, all of which employed a high-speed, two-cycle design, the H-Engine is a four-cycle design. Although it was developed independently of GE's 7HDL engine (see AC6000CW), Sean Graham-White in "6,000 h.p.," published in the January 1997 issue of

RailNews, points out that the two 6,000-horsepower engines share common characteristics, including dual turbochargers, electronic fuel injection, and a crankcase made of cast ductile iron. EMD's two-stroke engines use fabricated steel construction. Unlike General Electric, which worked with Deutz MWM in the development of its engine, EMD developed its H-Engine on its own. Electro-Motive's specifications indicate that the engine produces 6,300 brake horsepower working at 1,000 rpm: this translates to 6,000 horsepower available for traction. As reflected by its designation, the engine uses 16 cylinders with a 265x300-millimeter (10.4x11.4-inch) bore and stroke. By describing its engine in these metric measurements, Electro-Motive has abandoned its traditional practices of using English measurements and of designating its engines by volume cylinder displacement. EMD statistics indicate the H-Engine has about 1,010-ci displacement. Therefore, in traditional EMD engine terminology, the new engine would be described as a "16-1010."

The development, refinement, and practical application of the H-Engine took longer than originally planned. In anticipation of the new 6,000-horsepower engine, EMD introduced a temporary locomotive type: the "upgradeable" SD90MAC. As in the case of General Electric's AC6000CW described earlier, EMD built locomotives with the long platform and modern equipment capable of accepting its new engine, but delivered them with the older 16-cylinder 710G3B engine rated at just 4,300 horsepower. Electro-Motive lists this locomotive simply as "SD90MAC," while designating the "true" 6,000-horsepower locomotive as the SD90MAC-H, with the "H" signifying the big engine. Union Pacific, and other sources in the industry have variously called the "upgradeable" locomotive the "SD9043MAC," "SD90/43MAC," and "SD9043AC," with the "43" to reflect the 4,300-horsepower rating.

In recent years, the SD9043MAC has been the more common variation of the big locomotive on the road. Today, UP and Canadian Pacific are the primary users of the type. In 1999, CIT Group/Capital Finance ordered a fleet of 40 SD9043MACs for lease to North American railroads. These locomotives wear a maroon-and-gray livery with white, hashed nose stripes, and are lettered CEFX. They have been leased to a variety of railroads as the demand for power fluctuates.

The SD90MAC-H (according to EMD's published specifications) can deliver 200,000 pounds starting tractive effort and 170,000 pounds continuous tractive effort, making it the most powerful locomotive on the American market today. By comparison, GE's AC6000CW can produce 180,000 pounds starting tractive effort and 166,000 pounds continuous tractive effort.

To fulfill the goal of one 6,000-horsepower locomotive to replace every two 3,000-horsepower units in regular service, several impediments need to be addressed. An important concern for railroads is

Above: The back end of a Union Pacific SD90MAC (SD9043AC) 8090 shows the dynamic brake cabinet, cooling vents, and related machinery. *Tom Kline*

Above right: A pair of SD90MACs leads empty westbound coal hoppers though the junction at O'Fallons, Nebraska. This junction is where the Union Pacific's route to the Powder River diverges from the Overland Route. *Brian Solomon*

locomotive dependability. A 6,000-horsepower locomotive needs to be more dependable than lower-horsepower locomotives in order for the unit replacement equation to be cost effective. If one of four 3,000-horsepower locomotives fails on the road, a train will be able to limp along with three functional locomotives that represent 75 percent of the assigned horsepower. By contrast, if one of two 6,000-horsepower locomotives fails, a train has to get by with just half the assigned horsepower. This is a significant difference, especially considering that 6,000-horsepower locomotives are designed to handle some of the railroads' highest

priority trains. This not only delays the train with the failed locomotive but can also plug up an entire line, especially if the failure occurs on single track. While the practice of using single locomotives is more common than it once was, it is not a prevalent practice on American lines.

Another problem with very high-horsepower locomotives is their lack of flexibility. With such large blocks of power, railroads may find that they must either assign more power to a train than is really needed to move it over the road, or mix 6,000-horsepower units with other types—a practice that diminishes the power value of the big locomotives. In either case, the costs of using 6,000-horsepower units may exceed potential savings.

The large numbers of 4,000-horsepower and 4,400-horsepower locomotives ordered from both GM and GE since the mid-1990s in comparison with relatively conservative numbers of 6,000-horsepower locomotive orders indicate that the market for very-high-horsepower AC locomotives may be smaller than anticipated by the builders. Any new technology can pose unforeseen developmental difficulties, making it premature to disregard a new type because of early design problems. However, based on discussions with industry specialists, the future for 6,000 horsepower seems clouded as of 2002. Over the nearly 200-year history of locomotive development, numerous sound locomotive designs were prematurely condemned because of minor reliability problems in their early years. Likewise, a number of flawed designs touted as the power of the future were subsequently relegated as historical curiosities. If issues with 6,000-horsepower diesels are satisfactorily addressed, it will be interesting to see how the locomotive market responds to the development of the 6,000-horsepower single-engine diesel—and if locomotives with still higher ratings will eventually be developed.

Left: Big power in an unlikely place. In May 2000, a leased CEFX SD90MAC 138 leads Vermont Rail System train No. 263 eastbound at Ludlow, Vermont, on the former Rutland Railroad route over Mt. Holly. VRS experimented with AC traction, then later leased some DC traction SD70Ms from Susquehanna, before purchasing secondhand Texas-Mexican GP60s. *George S. Pitarys*

Below: Union Pacific 8500 Series SD90MAC-Hs lead a West Colton–to–Roseville, California, freight westward at the west switch of the Bealville siding in the California Tehachapis. These locomotives feature the big H-Engine, a four-cycle diesel designed for 6,000-horsepower output. *Dave Burton*

The 700 Series P32AC-DM appears very similar to Amtrak's other General Electric GENESIS types, the 800 Series DASH 8-P40Bs and 1 to 200 Series DASH 9-P42Bs (P42s for short). However, the 700 Series are quite different in several key respects. These locomotives use AC traction instead of DC, feature a 12-cylinder FDL engine instead of a 16-cylinder version, and are "dual-mode," equipped with retractable shoes for third-rail pickup in electrified territory. Amtrak's 700 Series are normally assigned to runs from Albany-Rensselaer down the Hudson to New York City's Penn Station. Metro-North also uses P32AC-DMs on its Grand Central–based suburban trains. Brian Solomon

25 General Electric
GENESIS

Drifting downgrade at Middlefield, Massachusetts, on July 19, 1997, this pair of GE P42s are almost silent as they roll toward Boston with train No. 448 on the Lake Shore Limited. Compare this view with the photo on page 13 of the same train at the same location made in the autumn

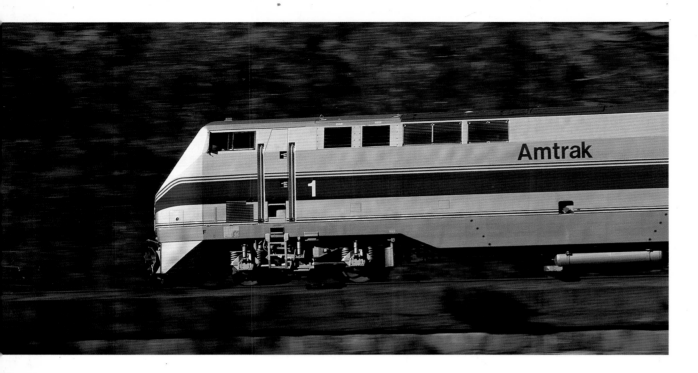

The General Electric GENESIS is unique in the annals of modern locomotives. Unlike all other modern locomotives, the GENESIS was specifically designed for North American passenger service. It is also unusual because, unlike modern freight locomotives, it uses a monocoque body style. Other modern American passenger locomotives, notably Amtrak's F40PH built by EMD beginning in 1976, were essentially adaptations of existing freight locomotive designs. (The F40PH is essentially a GP40-2 with a cowl body, high-speed gearing, and specialized equipment for passenger service, such as head-end power to provide heat and lighting on passenger cars.) In the early 1990s, Amtrak and General Electric engineers worked together to create an entirely new locomotive to meet Amtrak's specific needs. Amtrak wanted a powerful, lightweight locomotive without dimensional restrictions and a modern, forward-looking appearance.

To reduce locomotive weight, General Electric worked with Krupp, a German firm responsible for the high-speed ICE-1 body design, in the construction of a monocoque body to support the locomotive. Most modern American locomotives use a frame (sometimes called a "platform") as the locomotive support. With a monocoque design, the body shell is integrated in the locomotive structure. In this respect, GENESIS is like full carbody locomotives such as the EMD E- and F-Units built in the 1930s, 1940s, and 1950s. To comply with the most restrictive mainline clearances, the GENESIS is also lower and narrower than most North American locomotives. According to GE specifications, the GENESIS Series 1 is 14 feet, 6 inches tall, and 10 feet wide, making it a foot shorter and more than 2 inches narrower than most freight locomotives. Power for the new locomotive is a standard variation of GE's 7FDL prime mover rated at 4,000 horsepower.

The most striking quality of the GENESIS is the locomotive's unorthodox appearance—it doesn't look like anything else on American rails, past or present. According to articles by Bob Johnston in the September 1993 issue of *TRAINS* and David C. Warner in the June 1993 *Passenger Train Journal*, the GENESIS' appearance is a compromise afforded by Amtrak's specific desire for a modern look that is strong enough to withstand repeated grade crossing collisions, yet economical to build and repair. So by intent, the design uses a sharp, angular construction with flat surfaces free from curves that would be more costly to maintain. In its early years, the GENESIS design shocked many railroad observers and generated considerable criticism as a result of its nonconventional appearance. In August 1994, the readers of *Passenger Train Journal* voted GENESIS the "Ugliest-Ever Passenger Diesel." The opinion was not universally held—in the same poll, readers also listed GENESIS as the third-most "Attractive Passenger Diesel."

There are three basic variations of GENESIS diesels. The first are 4,000-horsepower locomotives built for Amtrak and designated DASH

Amtrak road No. 1 is a P42 GENESIS built by General Electric at Erie, Pennsylvania, in 1996. In October 2000, it lead Amtrak No. 449 on the westbound Boston section of the *Lake Shore Limited* at West Warren, Massachusetts. The locomotive is wearing Amtrak's short-lived *Northeast Direct* livery, which was discontinued with the introduction of the *Acela* livery in 2000. *Brian Solomon*

Amtrak No. 53 displays a variation of the *Acela* livery at Albany-Rensselaer Station in February 2002. The General Electric GENESIS has displaced the 1970s-era EMD F40PH as Amtrak's standard passenger locomotive. By the time this photograph was made, only a handful of F40PHs remained in service. *Brian Solomon*

8-40BPs by GE (sometimes listed as DASH 8-40BWHs) and P40s by Amtrak, and numbered in the 800 Series. This type debuted in 1993 and 44 were built at Erie between 1993 and 1994.

The more common GENESIS is the 4,200-horsepower P42DC that began production in 1996 and began with the Amtrak No. 1. Externally these locomotives look the same as the 800 Series GENESIS; the difference is that the P42DC uses DASH 9 technology while the DASH 8-40BP uses DASH 8 technology. The P42DCs have electronic fuel injection and other modern features that improved locomotive performance and reliability over the DASH 8 line. Both types use a 16-cylinder engine and conventional DC traction motors. In 2001, Canada's VIA Rail ordered a fleet of 21 P42DCs for its inter-city services.

The third variety of GENESIS, and by far the most unusual, is the P32AC-DM, a highly specialized machine designed for service on New York City's electrified lines. It is a dual-mode (thus the "DM" in the designation) locomotive that can either operate from its 12-cylinder 7FDL engine or can draw power from trackside DC third rail using retractable third-rail shoes. Unlike the other GENESIS models, the P32AC-DM uses AC traction motors. Both Amtrak and the suburban passenger carrier Metro-North operate fleets of P32AC-DMs. Amtrak's are numbered in the 700 Series and primarily used along the Hudson River line between the Albany-Rensselaer and New York City Penn Stations.

The GENESIS has been a great success. By 2001, most long-distance Amtrak trains outside the electrified Northeast Corridor were hauled by GENESIS locomotives. Locomotive engineer Craig Willett, who is known for his traditional preference for EMDs, says with a grin, "The P42 is making a GE person out of me! They're good engines with better creature comforts. They're quieter, and can make better time over the road than F40s. [They also] are about one-third more fuel efficient than an F40."

Two freshly painted GE P42s in Amtrak's latest livery lead train No. 4, the *Three Rivers*, eastbound at Summer Hill, Pennsylvania, on October 21, 2001. *T. S. Hoover*

BIBLIOGRAPHY

BOOKS

Alymer-Small, Sidney. *The Art of Railroading, Vol. VIII*. Chicago, 1908.

Armstrong, John H. *The Railroad: What it Is, What it Does*. Omaha, Neb., 1982.

Bruce, Alfred W. *The Steam Locomotive in America*. New York, 1952.

Burch, Edward P. *Electric Traction for Railway Trains*. New York, 1911.

Bush, Donald, J. *The Streamlined Decade*. New York, 1975.

Churella, Albert, J. *From Steam to Diesel*. Princeton, N.J., 1998.

Diemer, Hugo. *Self-Propelled Railway Cars*. Chicago, 1910.

Dolzall, Gary W., and Stephen F. Dolzall. *Baldwin Diesel Locomotives*. Milwaukee, Wis., 1984.

Drury, George H. *Guide to North American Steam Locomotives*. Waukesha, Wis., 1993.

Farrington, S. Kip, Jr. *Railroading the Modern Way*. New York, 1951.

Garmany, John B. *Southern Pacific Dieselization*. Edmonds, Wash., 1985.

Garrett, Colin. *The World Encyclopedia of Locomotives*. London, 1997.

General Motors. *Electro-Motive Division Operating Manual No. 2300*. La Grange, Ill., ca. 1945.

Haut, F. J. G. *The Pictorial History of Electric Locomotives*. Cranbury, N.J., 1970.

Herrick, Albert, B. *Practical Electric Railway Hand Book*. New York, 1906.

Hofsommer, Don. L. *Southern Pacific 1900–1985*. College Station, Tex., 1986.

Jennison, Brian, and Victor Neves. *Southern Pacific Oregon Division*. Mukilteo, Wash., 1997.

Keilty, Edmund. *Interurbans Without Wires*. Glendale, Calif., 1979.

Kirkland, John, F. *Dawn of the Diesel Age*. Pasadena, Calif., 1994.

Kirkland, John, F. *The Diesel Builders, Vols. I, II, and III*. Glendale, Calif., 1983.

Klein, Maury. *Union Pacific, Vol. II*. New York, 1989.

Marre, Louis A. *Diesel Locomotives: The First 50 Years*. Waukesha, Wis., 1995.

Marre, Louis A., and Jerry A. Pinkepank. *The Contemporary Diesel Spotter's Guide*. Milwaukee, Wis., 1985.

Marre, Louis A., and Paul K. Withers. *The Contemporary Diesel Spotter's Guide, 2000 Edition*, Halifax, Penn., 2000.

Middleton, William D. *When the Steam Railroads Electrified*. Milwaukee, Wis., 1974.

Mulhearn, Daniel J., and John R. Taibi. *General Motors' F-Units*. New York, 1982.

Pinkepank, Jerry A. *The Second Diesel Spotter's Guide*. Milwaukee, Wis., 1973.

Ransome-Wallis, P. *World Railway Locomotives*. New York, 1959.

Reagan, H. C., Jr. *Locomotive Mechanism and Engineering*. New York, 1894.

Reck, Franklin M. *On Time*. Electro-Motive Division of General Motors. Detroit, 1948.

Reck, Franklin M. *The Dilworth Story*. New York, 1954.

Signor, John R. *Donner Pass: Southern Pacific's Sierra Crossing*. San Marino, Calif., 1985.

Signor, John R. *The Los Angeles and Salt Lake Railroad Company*. San Marino, Calif., 1988.

Signor, John R. *Tehachapi*. San Marino, Calif., 1983.

Solomon, Brian. *The American Diesel Locomotive*. Osceola, Wis., 2000.

Solomon, Brian. *The American Steam Locomotive*. Osceola, Wis., 1998.

Solomon, Brian. *Locomotive*. Osceola, Wis., 2001.

Solomon, Brian. *Trains of the Old West*. New York, 1998.

Staff, Virgil. *D-Day on the Western Pacific*. Glendale, Calif., 1982.

Strapac, Joseph A. *Southern Pacific Motive Power Annual 1971*. Burlingame, Calif., 1971.

Strapac, Joseph A. *Southern Pacific Review 1953–1985*. Huntington Beach, Calif., 1986.

Strapac, Joseph A. *Southern Pacific Review 1981*. Huntington Beach, Calif., 1982.

Strack, Don. *Union Pacific 2000 Locomotive Directory*. Halifax, Penn., 2000.

Swengel, Frank M. *The American Steam Locomotive: Vol. 1, Evolution*. Davenport, Iowa, 1967.

Withers, Paul K. *Norfolk Southern Locomotive Directory 2001*. Halifax, Penn., 2001.

BROCHURES

Alco-Méditerranée S.A.R.L. *Alco 251 Diesels*. Paris. (No date.)

General Electric. *GE Locomotives*. (No date.)

General Electric. *GENESIS Series*. ca. 1993.

PERIODICALS

CTC Board. Ferndale, Wash.

Diesel Era. Halifax, Penn.

Extra 2200 South. (No date.)

Locomotive & Railway Preservation. Waukesha, Wis. (No longer published.)

Official Guide to the Railways. New York.

Pacific RailNews. Waukesha, Wis. (No longer published.)

Passenger Train Journal. Waukesha, Wis. (No longer published.)

Railroad History, formerly *Railway and Locomotive Historical Society Bulletin*. Boston, Mass.

Railway Gazette, 1870–1908. New York.

Southern Pacific Bulletin. San Francisco. (No longer published.)

TRAINS magazine. Waukesha, Wis.

Vintage Rails. Waukesha, Wis. (No longer published.)

INDEX